The Magic of the Kerry Coast

JOHN M. FEEHAN

THE MERCIER PRESS
CORK

The Mercier Press Limited
Cork

ISBN 978 1 78117 908 6

© John M. Feehan 1979.

Books by the same author:
THE WIND THAT ROUND THE FASTNET SWEEPS
TOMORROW TO BE BRAVE
AN IRISH PUBLISHER AND HIS WORLD

Transferred to Digital Print-on-Demand in 2024

DEDICATED TO
JOHANNA KEANE
MY YOUNG KERRY LOVE

INTRODUCTION

Some reviewers as well as many of the general public seemed to have been intrigued by my last book *The Wind that Round the Fastnet Sweeps* and to have found a little trouble in attempting to classify it. One came up with the rather unusual idea that it was an attempt to describe sailing to farmers; another thought it was nothing more than a drunken pub-crawl from harbour to harbour, making fun of everyone who happened to cross my path; someone else said it was a collection of falsehoods based on truths—I'm still trying to figure that one out—while yet another thought it was a deep spiritual search into the enigma of my own soul, and compared it, God help me, to the *Confessions of Saint Augustine*. Augustine was a reformed rake who had the best of both worlds—so far, I've had the best of neither—which makes the comparison meaningless. At the Listowel Writers Week our greatest dramatist, John B. Keane, described it as 'The Irish Story of San Michele'. Would to God that were true. Munthe's book is reported to have sold 50,000,000 copies and if mine only achieved an infinitesimal fraction of that sale, my creditors would be delighted, and I would be received with open arms into the great freemasonry of those who have the name of money and little else.

There is nothing mysterious about my book. I admit from time to time I venture into the nether world—that mysterious cloudy land between life and death. But I do so regularly and indeed there are times when I feel myself more at home there than I do here. *The Wind that Round the Fastnet Sweeps* is a simple travel book with no pretentions whatever to great literature. It is not that I didn't sit up night after night trying to weave sentences, searching for words, trying to make sense out of confused tumbling thoughts and to transfer that onto paper, but I was conscious all the time that I should not write about places but about people, including myself. It does not really matter what secrets a writer reveals of his own soul; one day they will be an open book to the entire human race and a man might as well make a start in this world. I did not try to make fun of the people I met. No man has the right to laugh at another, he only has the right to laugh with him, and I laughed a great deal with those who honoured me with their companionship. At times I tried hard to laugh at myself, but that is the greatest of all gifts, which God only bestows on his special friends.

The old matchmaker who wanted to fix me up with the stuttering widow is dead. One reviewer claimed he never existed. I only wish that critic could have been present on the cold bleak February day when the poor man was laid to rest, in a windswept mountainy graveyard, mourned by hundreds of couples whom he had so skilfully brought together. Yes, he was real alright but his kind has vanished forever. Different and more sophisticated techniques have now taken over.

The tinker has gone from success to success. Not so long ago a very large sum of money was stolen from his caravan but it didn't worry him. 'A thing of nothing,' he said, 'I'll have it made up in six months with the help of God and his blessed Mother.'

I have never come across the commercial traveller I met in Kinsale, but I'm told that since the book was published there has been an enormous increase in the number of men calling to caravan sites and welcoming the strangers on behalf of the Irish Government, and I suppose that cannot be but beneficial to our tourist industry.

I've had six letters from different women each stating that they were in the small rowing boat in Toormore Bay when I stood up naked in *Dualla* and waved to them. Each said that she was shocked at the time, but having read my book she fully understood and accepted my apologies, and would pray for me. Strange, I could only see two women in that boat that day, but it may be I'm getting old and my eyesight is failing.

The Wind that Round the Fastnet Sweeps ended in Crookhaven. *The Magic of the Kerry Coast* begins there. It follows the same pattern; a little sailing, a little thinking, a little laughing, a little drinking. It is not meant to instruct you, only to entertain, and perhaps give you a few hours of happiness and brightness in a life that is often desolate and dark. So cast off the tired ways of the city and we'll search together for those priceless moments of time when sea and sky and land blend into infinite beauty. We'll hoist the sails and venture out into the deep blue sea where the waves will jump and frolic, and where the soft west wind will ruffle the hair, caress the cheeks and sweep away all the sorrows and cares of a very lonely world.

J. M. F.
March 1979

1

We left Crookhaven in somewhat of a hurry just in case the police decided to pay us a courtesy call, as police sometimes do when they are unsure of the credentials of their customers. It happened this way: the two young companions, who were cruising with me, had taken a little more liquid refreshment than usual and at dusk the evening before they boarded an American yacht, which had just arrived in Ireland, and represented themselves as the two sons of the Lord Mayor of Goleen. Yes, they informed the strangers, Goleen was the third largest city in Ireland and had a corporation of aldermen and burgess for more than six centuries. Since this particular American yacht, they said, was the first to visit Crookhaven for several years the Lord Mayor had decided to confer the Freedom of the City on the occupants, and to give a luncheon in their honour at the guildhall, Goleen. This gesture of goodwill, it was explained, was a token of the esteem in which all Americans are held in Ireland. The visitors were therefore cordially invited to present themselves in Goleen the following day at twelve o'clock for the commencement of the ceremonies. The unfortunate Americans, four bearded males, fell for the story hook, line and sinker and so my two tricksters were dined and wined in a manner befitting their exalted lineage. As a parting gift they were given a large bottle of brandy and, in turn, they discreetly whispered a telephone number to the Americans where female accommodation was available. The ladies names were Allana and Mavourneen, and they would be most certain to please. It was bad enough that the telephone number so discerningly passed on was that of a well-known homosexual, but they put themselves dangerously outside the law when they finally, as a parting shot, exempted the Americans from all Customs examination. This alone carried a penalty of twelve months minimum with hard labour, so when we were leaving in the morning I thought it prudent to confine them to their quarters below, until we had at least cleared the Alderman Rocks and were well out to sea.

As *Dualla* was passing the American yacht I hailed them and asked if they were cruising east or west. East, they said, but they had first to attend a reception at the guildhall in Goleen and with all the expected festivities would not likely move out for a day or two. This was reassuring news. Since we were cruising to the west it was unlikely that our tracks would cross again, and so my two heroes were saved the necessity of hiding themselves in every port. I could not help wondering what these yachtsmen would think of Irish truth when they found out that Goleen was a tiny village of less than one hundred souls. When we were well clear of the dangerous Alderman Rocks, at the entrance to Crookhaven, and safely out of sight of the Americans, I called the two of them to take over *Dualla*. I collected a few cushions from the cabin and settled myself comfortably on the foredeck, with the mast as a back-rest and Maxie, my husky-alsatian dog, lying beside me, his magnificent furry head resting across my knees. It was a glorious day. The wind blew gently from the south. The morning sun was flirting with the glittering waves and descending on the sea like rays of silver dust. The caves on the shore were opening up to absorb the fresh brilliant light in the first flush of day. The blue of the sea was in harmony with the dome of the sky as *Dualla* sailed along, her course set for the tricky Dursey Sound, which was the gateway to all the beauty and magic of the Kerry coast. I am always a little lonely and a little sad when I leave Crookhaven because it is one of those harbours where a man can feel completely at home. It is a favourite port for cruising yachtsmen and it does not matter who you are, whether you have a broken-down boat or an expensive yacht, everyone gets the same treatment. The tinker is as welcome as the millionaire. Crookhaven has never lost its character or sold its soul. In the distant past Crookhaven was a port of life and activity, when the great sailing ships crossing the Atlantic called there for orders and supplies. It is said that in those days a man could walk the full length of the harbour merely by stepping from one ship to the other. Piracy and smuggling, those two great specialities of upright gentlemen, were part of its daily life. Indeed Crookhaven was the headquarters of a famous pirate called Nutt, who had three ships under his command, and who not only attacked the British merchant shipping, but also enriched himself by plundering the English coastal settlers. On the great principle that if you can't beat him buy him off, the London government gave Nutt a free pardon and a civil pension, more than he would have ever got if he stayed quietly at home by the fire, which shows that even in those days, like present-day Ireland, crime paid handsomely. It was in Crookhaven also that the press baron, Paul Reuter, had his first foreign station. Ships coming from America would drop a sealed container with dispatches off the Mizen Head. Local fishermen then retrieved this container, brought it to Reuters office from where the news was transmitted by telephone to the London newspapers. It was in this way that the first account of Lincoln's death reached the British press, before even the American ambassador knew of it. It made sensational headlines, and the British Government tried to have Reuter arrested and put on trial for spreading false information, but the arrival, later, of some transatlantic ships confirmed the truth of the news. Here, too, on nearby Brow Head, the great Marconi had one of his first radio stations. When poor Marconi explained to his friends and colleagues that he had discovered a principle by which he could send messages through the air without the aid of wires, they had him discreetly arrested and committed to a mental home for several days for observation. With the coming of steam, the famine, and the decline of fishing Crookhaven declined too: however, in the great West Cork resurgence of the past ten years it has come to life again, not as a centre of industry and shipping, but as a tourist attraction of rustic charm and beauty.

I particularly welcomed the light breeze and the clear fresh air of the morning, because my head was somewhat wheezy after the night before in Crookhaven. While the boys were being entertained by the Americans, I spent the evening in a crowded bar enjoying a concert of traditional music and song. Half-way through the session I was cornered by a tipsy Kerryman who talked almost non-stop, claiming to be an expert in all matters musical. Everyone in his family going back for generations were expert musicians, he boasted, and he knew every worthwhile player of the past fifty years. I listened to his torrent of words for more than an hour, and was about to move away from him to a more congenial corner, when he asked me had I ever heard of the great Connie Coorloon. I admitted that I hadn't.

'Connie,' he said, 'was a cousin of me great-grandfather, and he lived back in Kerry before the turn of the century, and what I'm going to tell you now you never heard of before. You see, all them great singers like Caruso and McCormack had their vocal chords in their throats, but Connie went one better. He had his situated in his backside, if you please. Yes—right there in his behind, and even when he was a child, he could sound the nicest notes you ever heard in your born life, nicer than any trumpet. This became a class of hobby with him, don't you see, and when he was growing up he thought he might as well make the best use of his talents. He practised doh, ray, mee, fah, soh, and be God, after a while he was able to play *Three Blind Mice* and *Twinkle, Twinkle Little Star* and a lot more lively tunes too. He was the talk of the countryside, and whenever there'd be a crowd of men gathered together Connie wouldn't be a bit shy to perform. And what's more than that, he could keep going for up to twenty-minutes non-stop.

'But how could he manage enough wind for that length of time?' I asked sceptically.

'It was in the eat'n, don't you see. He'd get a couple of pounds of onions, a couple of pounds of spuds, a half-skillet of yella meal, and he'd boil them all together in a mash, and then wash them down with a half-gallon of buttermilk, and an hour after that he could keep going to beat the band. But the poor fellow died young, the Lord have mercy on him. I suppose it must have been the heavy strain on his innards. It was just as well, anyway, for the priests got up against him and read him off the altar once or twice. It wasn't that they minded too much in the beginning, but when he started performing at wakes and funerals and confirmations they had to call a halt. I suppose they thought it was disrespectful. Oh I often heard the ould people tracing about him. I bet you never heard the like of that now. Well if ever you're in south Kerry ask any ould crabbed farmer that would have a mind to talk and I bet you he heard tell of Connie Coorloon!' I have asked a few Kerry farmers if they knew of Connie and I've got a typical Kerry answer. 'I might have, but I don't remember.'

Dualla was now dancing her way through a sparkling sea that looked as if it had rained drops of sunlight throughout the night. The tide was ebbing and a soft wind blowing from the south was charming the waves. This wild turbulent corner, the scene of so many shipwrecks, today looked like an oasis of peace. Inside me lay a shoreline of unrivalled beauty, the Mizen Head, Three Castles Head and Muntervara Head, jutting out into the Atlantic in all their splendour and majesty. Ireland from the sea is as God created it. Ireland from the land is as man despoiled it. I feel that at this point I should warn all yachtsmen not to be taken in by my description of conditions as they were on this superb day. What we were experiencing was quite abnormal. The tidal race off the Mizen Head can be one of the worst in Europe and a lot of the time is impassable for small boats. With a tide against a wind in anything over force four it becomes quite dangerous. The race can extend virtually the whole way from Brow Head to Muntervara Head, a distance of six or seven miles, and is at its worst between the Mizen Head and Three Castles Head. I was once caught in this race in a tide that ran against a wind not quite force four, and it is one of the few experiences of my seafaring life that I do not ever want to remember. It took us four to five hours to cover a distance that should be covered in two, and we thought that each wave, as it pounded us mercilessly, would be our last. There is only one safe thing to do, and that is to travel when the wind is with the tide and to keep at least four miles off the heads which are easily recognisable from a long way out to sea. There are not three Castles on the head that bears this name, there is only one castle with three turrets—a gloomy old building which almost bathes its feet on a lake inhabited only by wild birds. If you are interested in ghosts make a note to visit this eerie spot. The last occupant at the end of the century was a proud widow called O'Donoghue. One day her three sons went forth on horseback and late that evening the riderless horses returned. She knew they got into a fight somewhere and got themselves killed. In her grief she took all the valuable paintings, gold, silver, priceless *objets d'art* from the castle and threw them into the lake. When she had it emptied of everything portable, she plunged in herself, and drowned. But the old people say that her spirit still haunts the place and would warn off any curious visitor who might try to recover the treasure.

A lot of the land around this beautiful and picturesque corner is now being bought up by Dutch and German investors, and in another twenty years, so an old man told me, an Irishman in West Cork will be as scarce as an Indian in Manhattan. I asked one of these speculators what the attraction was: 'Apart from the beauty of the scenery,' he answered, 'most continentals now live in fear of Euro-Communism. If these people get into power they will be no different from the Russians, and Europe will become one vast slave-camp. Any continental who can afford to do so is buying land well away from home, so that at least he will have somewhere to go to when this day of reckoning comes.'

As I lay back on *Dualla's* deck in a state of pleasant languor, enjoying the tranquility of the air and the subdued whispering sound of the water gently breaking on her bow, I overheard a discussion between my two young friends in the cockpit—now fully awake and composed—which thoroughly fascinated me. I should explain that these two young men—they were only students—who came with me, were, despite their pranks, a delight to sail with. Unfortunately a lot of our younger yachtsmen know nothing about cruising and are obsessed with that childish pastime of yacht racing in order to make themselves feel important. Not so with my two young friends. When they go sailing, they go for the sheer thrill and enjoyment of the trip. It does not matter to them whether they are in a leaking pookaun with a Connemara fisherman, or in the most expensive yacht built. The subject of their conversation on this beautiful day was a discussion on the economic, social and political consequences of adherence to the ten commandments. In other words what would happen to the world if everybody kept strictly and faithfully to each and everyone of the commandments? They foresaw total chaos on every level. *Thou shalt not kill*—this would mean the end of war, the total disbandment of all armies, the complete close-down of all munition works, throwing millions on the unemployment queue. *Thou shalt not steal*—there would be no work for banks, police, locksmiths, auditors, accountants and all others whose livelihood depends on the dishonesty of their fellow-men. *Thou shalt not commit adultery*—strict adherence to this would have a disastrous effect on motels, expensive restaurants, airlines, furriers, jewellers, and all who contribute in any way to keeping the other woman's mouth shut. *Thou shalt not bear false witness against thy neighbour*—adherence to this commandment would virtually close down the legal profession, the insurance business, newspapers, TV-studios, politicians and all those who depend on stretching the truth for their existence. The mind boggles at the chaos that could result. They estimated that more than two thirds of the world's work force would be unemployed, millions would starve to death each year, and the world would be in a constant state of famine and pestilence. They finally came to the conclusion that sin was an absolute necessity if the world population were to survive. The lesson they learned from this speculation was, that as human beings, they would be seriously neglectful of the welfare of their fellow men, if they did not contribute to the common good in some way by a moderate amount of sinning. A few lies here and there, a little dishonesty in the matter of tax and insurance, a spot of adultery now and then to keep tuned up, would all help the good of mankind. After all, they argued, if God made us the way he did, he would never clap us up for all eternity because one got oneself mixed up with a pretty pair of legs; and in support they quoted the great Omar Khayyam:

> *Ah, Thou who didst with pitfall and with Gin*
> *Beset the road I was to wander in*
> *Thou wilt not with predestination round*
> *Enmesh me and impute my fall to sin.*

Inside us as we sailed along lay one of the most beautiful and picturesque corners of Ireland: Dunmanus bay with its majestic mountains and cliffs running sheer into the sea, with its sad memories of the famine and the thousands who died on its shores, and Bantry Bay set in the tropical hinterland of the beautiful Glengarriff woods and mountains. This corner of Ireland is a corner of memories and sadnesses, a territory that brought forth a people who were never to yield, and who for centuries were to endure the savageries and cruelties of the occupying forces, until freedom dawned for them at last. But I do not see it only as a place of bloody battles and massacres, I see it primarily as an area where the light of learning and culture was kept alive, despite the most barbarous oppression, for it was in Kerry and West Cork that the famous Irish hedge schools flourished. Let me explain: Ireland was once the centre of learning and culture in Europe. Thousands of students from all over the continent came to attend her great universities at Clonmacnoise, Clonard, Lismore and many other centres. After the British occupation of the country every Irish educational establishment was closed down, and in the words of the

English historian Lecky, the legislation on Irish education 'amounted simply to universal, unqualified and unlimited proscription'. Irish professors and teachers were imprisoned, fined and sometimes executed. Substantial rewards were offered and given to those who brought about their capture, and from this arose an army of spies and informers, like the old bounty hunters of the west, who infested the countryside. Because the people wanted an education and the schoolmasters were willing to risk their lives, there grew up a type of clandestine school which came to be known as the hedge school and which was to have a profound influence, not only on the cultural life of the nation, as it kept alive the spirit of learning and scholarship, but also on the political life of the nation insofar as these schools became the cradle of the rebellions and revolutions that were to follow in later years. Because the law was so severe these brave and defiant schoolmasters had to teach secretly, and so if the weather was fine they selected, in some remote glen, a sunny spot sheltered by a high hedge, and there sitting on a stone or stump of tree, the hunted schoolmaster taught his little school. This is how they came to be known as 'hedge' schools. Of course if the weather was bad he used some rough shelter made of wattles, stones and mud, and all the while, up on a high tree or hill, one or two of the pupils were posted as sentries to warn on the approach of an informer. Each pupil paid approximately five shillings per quarter to the schoolmaster who supplemented his meagre earning by doing casual work for farmers. One contemporary writer wrote:

> All over the country are numbers of schools where the lower orders have their children instructed in writing, artithmetic and reading; scarcely a peasant who can muster a crown but is emulous to expend it on his child's education.

And about the same time Lord Wakefield wrote:

> The people of Ireland are, I may almost say, univer-

sally educated. I do not know any part of Ireland so
wild that its inhabitants are not anxious and eager for
the education of their children.

The main subjects taught in these schools were Irish, arithmetic, French, Latin and Greek. The classics were particularly important because of the numbers being smuggled abroad to pursue their education in the universities of Europe. French was also a vital subject, since so many males left Ireland and joined the French army to fight against the British. Contemporary historians, like Smith, and travellers like Carr, have written with astonishment at the large numbers of impoverished and ragged peasants who could speak Irish, French, Latin and Greek fluently, but no English.

When I was a boy I knew an old man, then in his nineties whose only education was at a hedge school, but there was little about the ways of the world that he did not know. He was a man of great wealth who, as a youth, went into the contracting business and concentrated on supplying the British military barracks with fodder for the horses. To preserve anonymity we shall call him Murphy, though that was not his name. Murphy, being a true Irishman, felt that the British army was there for the picking. By an ingenious system of gratuities and bribes, he arranged that most of the loads of hay, straw and turnips he delivered to the barracks went out a backway, and were re-delivered again so that he got paid many times over for each load. After almost half a century of this lucrative business some suspicion began to creep in concerning the source of Murphy's wealth, and to satisfy themselves that everything was in order the British government sent over a general and two colonels from the war office, to hold a court of enquiry into supposed irregularities in the supply of fodder to Her Majesty's horses. The court sat for over a week hearing all kinds of witnesses but in the end could find no real evidence to support the suspicion. Murphy was in the witness-box for nearly three hours and he managed to answer every question satisfactorily without really saying anything. A number of times during the cross-examination he was asked a particularly penetrating question. In order to give himself time to think out the answer he slowly addressed the court: 'Your Honour, Sir General,' he said, 'I don't rightly follow the question. You must understand that I'm a man who got very little education when I was young because we were so poor. I could never burn the candle at the two ends nor ring the chapel bell for two funerals. We were always caught between the mouth of the river and the tide. The only bit of learning I got was at a small hedge school on the Big Mountain!' By the time he said this, and the question was repeated, he had thought out the answer. Exasperated the court allowed him to stand down, but as he was leaving the room the president, who seems to have been a man not entirely devoid of humour, called after him: 'I say Murphy! Where did you say you were educated?'

'Oh, Your Honour, Sir General, at a small hedge school near the Big Mountain.'

'The Big Mountain,' repeated the general slowly, as he wrote it down. 'Thank you, Murphy, I would very much like to send my son there.'

Time has a habit of slipping by far too quickly in the presence of great beauty, and the early afternoon was upon us as we sailed in towards the Dursey Sound, at the tip of the wild indented Beara coastline, with its bleak rocks, flinty shores and swirling tumbling tides that never seem to sleep. Away to the west we could see the rocks known as Bull, Cow and Calf. The lighthouse on the Bull Rock was the last sight of Ireland for the hundreds of thousands of starving emigrants as they made their way to a new world and new hope. Few of them returned. Its flashing light said more goodbyes than words of welcome. There is a strange story told about how the Bull Rock got its name. It appears that a lady called Duban had an incestuous relationship with her father, a chieftain, Cairbre. Such things were not uncommon in those far off days of liberated morals. The result of this moment of joy was twins, one of whom was called Cork. Now Cork was taken by a druid to Beare Island and there he was tied to a bull's back and washed and washed for the best part of a year until all his inherited sinfulness was washed into the bay. When all this was over the bull took an almighty leap and landed in the sea way out beyond the Dursey Island, where he was immediately turned into a rock and underneath the rock is the first gate to hell. Cork became such a great saint that the whole county was called after him. The story that this was the gateway to the nether-world was given great credence when the captain of a British frigate happened to be in the vicinity, and saw four Dursey Island fishermen fishing from a small rowing boat. It was in the bad old days of the pressgang and the captain could not miss an opportunity of capturing four good men for His Majesty's navy. He lowered a boat with an officer and six sailors, who immediately gave chase. The Durseymen rowed for all they were worth and were seen disappearing into a huge cavern under the Bull Rock. The naval boat followed them and more than an hour passed without a sign of either boat reappearing. The captain sent a second boat and this too failed to return. Completely bewildered the captain came to the conclusion that the place was full of evil spirits and was really the gate of hell, so he hoisted sail and put under way as fast as he could . What really happened was that the Durseymen once inside the cavern climbed on ledges where there were huge boulders, and as each boat came in they dropped these boulders which smashed the boats and they then dealt speedily with any sailors who escaped drowning. When the coast was clear they emerged safely and returned to their island homes. Another incident which gave credence to this tradition concerned Finn McCool. Finn had a dwarf who was anxious to get married and settle down, so the Fianna searched all Ireland to find a suitable wife for him, but none was to be had since he would only marry one of his own height and size. Finally they located one called Blanaid on the Bull Rock. She was crying her eyes out for she had come from the other world. Since she was the right size the dwarf fell in love with her, and they were married in City-Cow-Titty on the Dingle peninsula, and they lived happily ever after under the Bull Rock.

The Dursey Sound is a narrow channel somewhat more than a mile long, and it separates Dursey Island from the mainland. It is one of the critical hazards facing any yachtsman sailing up the west coast. The tide rushes through, at up to four knots, and if there is an opposing wind of any strength there can be savage seas at either entrance—seas which run amok and shoot up, hissing like a serpent and breaking one upon the other in wild confusion, and at times serious enough to sink a small boat instantly. When we arrived there we found them reasonably calm, but trembling quietly like a wild animal sleeping uneasily. We had so planned our trip to arrive there at low water when the flow of the tide is at its weakest, but this had its own drawback. At the narrowest part of the channel and almost in the centre there is a dangerous rock with only two feet of water over it, so as we sailed in I thought it best to start up the engine in order to get that extra bit of power and control. As well, it often happens that one meets a different wind at the north entrance, and sometimes this is strong enough to sweep a boat straight on to the rock. So we half sailed, half motored through the sound, keeping close to the steep island cliffs were there is an adequate depth. Any fears that we might have had proved groundless. Inside us we could see the swirl of the tide over the rock, but there were no confused seas and the wind still blew regularly from the south, so when we were well clear of the north entrance, which was our exit, we turned off the engine and set course for Scariff Island which rises up near the entrance to Derrynane Harbour.

Every time I pass through the Dursey Sound I am overcome with a deep feeling of gloom and depression, even on the most beautiful of days. This is a kind of throw-back to a day long ago when I was a mere youth on an educational tour of this wild area, and my impressionable mind first learned of a measure that was enacted here which would be hard to equal in the annals of any country. When the English, under Mountjoy and Carew, were plundering the Beara peninsula, some of the inhabitants, mainly the old, the sick, women and children, sought refuge on Dursey Island. They were pursued by a detachment of English troopers, under one Broderick, who made a landing on the island and dragged every mortal one of these helpless people to the edge of the cliffs, put them to the sword, and flung their mangled bodies over the jagged rocks. The soldiers ran along the tops of the cliffs with screaming babies impaled on their swords, shouting with glee as they flung the innocent little bodies into the waters of the sound. In this way over three hundred helpless Irish women and children died the most appalling deaths. A contemporary witness describing the scene said that the whole sound ran red with the blood of the victims. Two weeks later the Irish garrison defending Dunboy Castle were assured that their lives would be spared if they surrendered. This they did because they were heavily outnumbered. No sooner, however, had they laid down their arms than every man of them was marched to the square in Castletownbere and mercilessly slaughtered. The people of the Beara peninsula have long memories, and they talk today with bitterness of these events as if they only happened recently. Near the hangman's house one speaks quite naturally of the rope.

When we cleared the Dursey Sound the whole magnificent panorama of the Kingdom of Kerry unfolded itself in all its beauty. There is something bewitching about this breathtaking vista. One after another, as if to welcome us, the islands loomed up from the liquid acres of wave and water, Deenish, Scariff, Moylaun and far out to sea, the Great Skellig set like a gigantic jewel in a sky of resplendent blue, and dominating all, the mountains of Kerry, deep in purple heather, each peak shyly peeping out from behind another. The sun poured out upon the myriad colour of land and sea a soft tenderness that touched the heart like fairy music. A wind full of cheerfulness and friendship filled our sails and the white foam from *Dualla's* prow sprang forth like the hawthorn blossoms bursting in the spring. There was a time in my life when great beauty quickened the heart to sorrow, made me sad and tinged with pain.

> *The beauty of this world hath made me sad*
> *This beauty that will pass...*

But as the years roll on I am beginning to feel myself more at one with the experience of beauty, for beauty does not die or fade away. What our dimmed eyes can now see, and our exhausted hearts feel, is but a foretaste of a beauty and a peace beyond all telling, like a little ray of sunshine falling across a prison cell, speaks to the prisoner of the brilliant absolute light of the sun.

> *Ah! but if mine had been the painter's hand*
> *To tell what then I saw, and add the gleam,*
> *The light that never was, on sea or land,*
> *The consecration and the poet's dream.*

I had taken over the wheel to give the two boys a rest, and on this beautiful day they went down into the cabin, lay on the bunks and fell asleep. I found this rather hard to understand. They slept by day when they should be awake, and they were awake by night galavanting the countryside when they should be asleep. It was on the tip of my tongue to make a pompous remark about youth but I restrained myself when I remembered that at their age I did exactly the same.

The county of Cork was gliding quickly past us and very soon we would be in Kerry waters. Did you ever hear how Kerry got its name? Well, there was this Queen of Connaught called Maeve who, if what they tell me is true, was by no means noted for the virtue of holy purity. She met a bit of a playboy whose name was Fergus and he spent a night with her in case she'd be lonesome, for her husband was away. Anyway the result of this night's consolation was triplets. One of these triplets, when he became a man, made his way south with an army and took over the area known as Trughanacney. His name was Ciar, and so he re-named it

Ciar-Rioghact—the Kingdom of Ciar, which of course translated means the Kingdom of Kerry. Or so the old people say, anyway.

The journey from the Dursey Sound to Derrynane is a short one and with the light wind blowing it was a matter of less than two hours, and so after a delightful spell on the wheel, as *Dualla* drew close to Moylaun Island, I had to hail my two companions and awaken them from their short-lived sleep. The entrance to Derrynane can be very tricky because of its narrowness, just a few boat lengths wide, and on each side there are jagged dangerous rocks, which make it essential not to deviate anything from the marked course. We thought it best therefore to drop all sail outside and motor in, and when we had passed the starboard beacon at the end of Lamb Island, we dropped anchor in two fathoms of crystal clear water in the most beautiful harbour imaginable, sheltered from every wind, surrounded by islands and purple hills, perfumed by the sensuous scent of heather, honeysuckle and wild woodbine. Virgil must have had a vision of Derrynane harbour when he wrote:

> *There is a bay whose deep retirement hides*
> *The place where nature's self a port provides,*
> *Framed by a friendly islands jutting sides,*
> *Bulwark from which the billows of the main*
> *Recoil upon themselves, spending their force in vain.*

2

When we had the sails stowed, the deck tidied up and the punt launched, my companions set about two enterprises which always engage their urgent attention the moment we arrive in a new harbour. The first of these is to scan the surrounding terrain with field-glasses to 'spot form', to see if there are any lonely or forsaken looking females in sight who might be in need of a little male gallantry during our stay. At first this might appear a very romantic gesture, but for men of the sea it can have solid practical undertones in a harbour like Derrynane. The nearest village where supplies can be had is Caherdaniel, a long three mile walk, and while it is nice to make attractive friends during a stay, it becomes still nicer if those winsome friends happen to have a car. The second matter, though of lesser importance, is to see if there are any lone punts near the pier. On *Dualla* we carry only one punt and, since we are not likely to be engaged in the same nightly activities, the chances are that we would be returning to the yacht at different times, so it is always quite convenient if we can find an obliging fisherman or resident willing to loan us his punt. This is usually not a great problem as most local owners do not use theirs after dark.

It was not too long before a few prospects were spotted so the two quickly rowed ashore to make contact while I stayed on board to prepare an evening meal. They brought Maxie with them since he, too, needed to make a few contacts on land. In less than an hour they returned, accompanied by two very attractive young German girls who, they said, with a wink, would like to join us for an evening meal. The wink told me that the girls owned a car. We all sat down and opened two bottles of wine to help us with the cold table I had already prepared, and the conversation started rolling. The girls were holidaying in Ireland and spending a few days around and about Derrynane. They really loved Ireland, they said. It was a dream island, a paradise. What attracted them most was a combination of isolation, beautiful landscape and the friendliness of the people. Unfortunately the continent was overcrowded. A place like Derrynane would have several major hotels, a casino or two, and every beach would be thronged. In Ireland one had a sense of freedom. Did they not think we were too isolated? Oh, no. One can never be too isolated on a holiday. The Irish people, they thought, were wonderful, kind, generous, honest, sincere. They could not praise us enough. I pointed out rather gingerly that while everything they said about us was true, the exact *opposite* was also true. We were mean, treacherous, unreliable, double-faced and were not to be trusted too far. They hadn't run into these qualities, they had only seen the nicer sides. As they drank more wine they became coyly inquisitive. Were we married? No. I was a widower. Were the two boys my sons? No, only friends. Did we sail a lot? Yes, all summer. Did we ever work? Yes, sometimes in winter. Would I get married again? I said there was nothing much against it, neither was there much for it. In matters of love, I said, men are like sheep at a fair—the women are the buyers. Would they like to marry an Irishman and live in Ireland? Oh, yes, they would very much. They had fallen in love with Ireland and now all that remained was to fall in love with two Irishmen. This light-hearted conversation went on right through the meal, a mixture of banter, drollery and merriment. When they were standing up afterwards and about to leave they began speaking German to each other while I was clearing the table and the boys making themselves ready.

'I think there are possibilities here. They seem a decent lot.'

'I like the widower. It's a pity he's so old.'

'I wouldn't trust him too far. When he looks at you he takes off your clothes with his eyes.'

'The two young lads look a bit uneasy but I suppose we had better settle for them. They're more our own age.'

German is one of the languages I speak fluently so I understood every word they said. Outside on deck I helped them one by one into the punt.

'Are you not coming with us?' asked the younger demurely.

'No, I'm not,' I answered, now in perfect German. 'I like to read German lyrical poetry in the evenings. I have a beautiful anthology with me.' I blew a kiss at them and dropped into the cabin before they had time to recover.

An hour later I had tidied up and I came out on deck to sit a while and enjoy the calm and peace of the lingering summer evening. There was a mysterious stillness all around me. The scarlet sun was saying goodnight to day, and slowly lowering itself at the other end of the world. The dappled sky had the appearance of a red and purple coloured bedspread. On the shore the gorse and heather poured forth their sweet and delicate perfume and scattered it through the air, like rays of gold, which sent a feeling of intoxication through the body, a vague longing for something wondrous and permanent. All was so tranquil and hushed. It was that miraculous moment when heaven meets earth hushing the sounds of the world, and soothing the sorrows of this enigmatic life.

In the making of films there is a technique whereby the screen seems to quiver, shake and dissolve, producing a flashback to events of the past, and I thought, if the enchanting scene before me now were to melt into the past and jump the bridge of two hundred years, what would I see? A stately mansion, Derrynane House, home of the O'Connells, hidden in the woods at the foot of the hills in the wildest and most remote part of Ireland. The harbour would be full of fishing craft, but in their midst discreetly anchored, I would see one or two forty ton cutters, with French names, resting, having discharged their cargoes of smuggled goods, and awaiting a cargo of Irishmen to join the French army and young students to continue their studies in Paris. Up above at the Great House the O'Connells would be sitting down to supper with thirty or forty retainers. This great family managed to hold on to Derrynane during the penal days, when all property was forbidden to Catholics, by a device, where one of their kinsmen, Hugh Falvey, not too scrupulous about religious matters, became a Protestant and bought land for the O'Connells. Later, when the British officials challenged Hugh on this he replied: 'I am ready to swear the print out of the bible that I bought the lands for myself.' When Hugh was getting old he was asked by 'Hunting Cap' O'Connell, the great Dan's uncle, to buy another bit of land for the family near Killarney. Old Hugh wrote in reply: 'My dear Maurice, if I were a few years younger I would be ready to oblige a friend as ever. I regret I am too near my end to perjure myself any more even for so old and valued a friend as yourself.' He was a prudent man and he felt as death approached it might be no harm to keep an odd eye on the next world. Unfortunately he did not get too much warning. One night a couple of soldiers broke into his house and tried to abduct his daughter. He managed, with the help of his son John to beat them off, but in the scuffle old Hugh noticed that one of the robbers was missing a finger. Some weeks later a man named Sullivan, who was also missing a finger, was arrested, tried and hanged. In fact, Sullivan was completely innocent and had nothing to do with the break-in. His sister, wild with grief, publicly cursed Hugh and John at a fair in Cahirsiveen, and called on all the gods in heaven to give them a sudden death. Not long afterwards old Hugh was found dead in his own yard and John was killed when he fell from a horse. The fortunes of the O'Connell family were built up almost entirely on smuggling to and from France and Spain. The incoming cargoes were mainly tea, sugar, tobacco, rum, brandy, clarets, silks, satins and velvets and, perhaps most important of all, a priest or two who had just been ordained. The returning cargo would consist of butter, lards, fish, linen and wool, but the greater part of the little vessels would be taken up by Irishmen, those Wild Geese, going out to join the French army to strike a blow against their ancient enemy, the English. Daniel O'Connell's grandmother, Marie Dubh, saw her sons and eighteen of her relatives sail out of Derrynane to join the Wild Geese, and as she said goodbye she pleaded with them to return one day to free their country. Marie Dubh, the mother of twenty-two children, was a hard tough woman, not to be trifled with. Once, when a paid informer was about to give evidence that she was a Catholic, she asked her followers to prevent him from doing so but not to kill him. They obeyed her orders to the letter and promptly cut his tongue out. Smuggling was brought to a fine art by the O'Connells and their kinsmen in this wild lonely corner of Kerry. A very thorough system of signals from headland to headland was in operation, and when a suspicious sail was sighted calculations were made as to where it was likely to be at nightfall. A horse with a lantern tied around its neck was then put grazing in a field near the shore. The up-and-down movement of the lantern fooled the suspected ship into believing that the light came from the cabin of a vessel and there was open water in that direction. Thinking this to be so the crew steered inwards and were dashed to pieces on the rocks—a grim warning to strange sail not to come too near Derrynane. As well, no customs official would dare come too close to the harbour because he knew the chances of his returning were slim. Morgan O'Connell was once tried for his life on a charge of practically murdering one such customs officer who caught him landing a cargo of contraband. After a short absence a Protestant jury acquitted this Catholic gentleman. They were all his best customers. But while the great lived well the ordinary Irishman eked out a most miserable existence. The magnificent woods, blue with wild hyacinths, and the hillsides yellow with gorse hid the wretched thatched-roofed hovels of the poor. Ragged, hungry and frozen they clung to life from hour to hour and day to day on the verge of starvation and death. The snug and prosperous little farm houses, with their fields of golden corn gently sweeping down to the gnarled rugged shore, is the refreshing sight that meets the eye today. Gone are the spectres of misery, destitution and want, and with them the barbaric times when to be an Irishman was to be but one little step above an animal.

Dusk was now creeping over the earth. The cloudless sky was folding itself into night, and the twilight was blending with the darkness. A pale moon began to glide stealthily over the horizon looking for all the world like the face of death. The stars, which Byron called the poetry of heaven, appeared one by one and seemed as if they were dancing in the water. Memories began to tumble in on my mind—those memories that cause a stab of pain mingled with a shaft of joy. I went into the cabin and settled down to sleep. Maxie

coiled himself up at the foot of my bed and kept gazing at
me with his sad mournful eyes. I slept soundly and never
even heard the boys returning.

Because we were very tired after the long run we slept
late in the morning. The wind had risen during the night
and was now blowing strongly from the south. It was
almost midday by the time our breakfast was over and the
boys had arranged to meet the German girls on shore. They
had generously offered to take us in their car shopping to
Caherdaniel which was only a little over three miles away.
When we rowed ashore I took Maxie for a run and then
returned to the pier. The girls greeted me with most beguiling smiles and had obviously forgotten the little *faux pas* of
the evening before. Did I sleep well during the night? Yes, I
did, very well. Was I not lonely by myself on the boat? Yes,
I was, but loneliness has its compensations. What were
they? Peace of mind. Could I not have peace of mind with
a companion? Yes, of course—but I had a companion whom
I loved very much, Maxie. Did I prefer his company to that
of humans? Yes. I did most of the time. At this they were
taken aback but when I assured them that I much preferred
their company, they laughed gaily again, really not knowing
whether to believe me or not but still giving me the benefit
of the doubt. In Caherdaniel I went into a delightful well-
stocked shop while the others strolled off to post some
cards to their friends. Later, when I had my purchases made
I dropped into a pub to sample the ale. There I ran into an
old friend of mine, Larry the Liar, a tinker who dealt in
scrap. I had known Larry for twenty years or more, and in
my travels throughout the country since then I often ran
into him in the most unexpected places. The first time I
met him was in a town up the midlands when he was hiding
from the police. He was wanted for questioning in connection with the disappearance of a pigs head from a butcher's
shop. He also removed a pair of new stockings from the
parish priest's clothes line, and left his own stinking ones
instead. He maintained it was fair exchange, although he

afterwards admitted there was a slight betterment on his side. I hid him in the back of the car, covered with a rug, and drove him out of the town to safety. Since then we were fast friends. Larry, now in his late seventies, was a tall angular man with a bruised and battered face, partly hidden by a large walrus moustache, a pair of long legs so out of joint that they looked like two crooked gate posts. He was alone in the world now since his wife died.

'Well, by the Lord Jaysus, is it yourself is in, Sean?' he shouted. ''Tis a cure for sore eyes to see you. Where are you eatin' the pigs head this weather? Sit up there on the stool and we'll have a ball of malt together for ould times sake.' The drinks were ordered and we began to chat in the way old friends do when they haven't met for a long time. He was doing well with the scrap now, he said, and was able to buy plenty of food for himself and put a few shillings by every week for the price of a coffin and a High Mass when he died. Sure no matter how bad the times were in the past he always knew that the apples would grow again and the hunger clear away over the tops of the mountains. There's no use complaining or talking about the noise when the thunder is gone, he said. Things are easier now for when you have a loaf of bread 'tis easy to find a knife to cut it. All his twelve children had gone and most of them were married. The eldest has his own caravan and makes a good living sellin' linoleum and carpets to farmers. The youngest has a great job below in the north killin' fowl and pluckin' feathers for a butcher. A class of a butcher's undertaker, he added with a grin. Wasn't it great that he could afford a new tent last year? You'd want a good tent when you're gettin' ould for the winter wind is so sharp that 'twould go through a coffin of American oak. The new tent was bone dry—as dry, he said, as a sermon of last Mass on a Sunday. He didn't mix much now with the other tinkers, nor bother to go to Puck or Cahermee fairs, for they were always fighting and rowing. They'd be sharin' the crame of the milk with one another today, and tearin' the shirts off their backs tomorrow.

'Them rich fellows that does be doin' good wanted me to go into a house,' he said, "'twas a grand place with a bath and a shit-house inside out of the rain. But sure what the hell would I want with a pot for me arse in me ould age? I'm using the ditches and headlands of Ireland now for seventy years and I may as well keep givin' them my custom 'till I die. Me hair is too grey to change me ways now.'

'But wouldn't you like to have an odd bath now and again?' I asked him.

'Yerra, bath me behind,' he replied. 'What would the likes of me want a bath for? I fell into a drain wanst when I was runnin' from a bailiff and that bath did me for the rest of me life.' Larry may have looked like a tramp, but his conversation excelled that of a king. When the boys and girls joined us his eyes sparkled with life and he almost danced with delight. He called for drinks all round, went over to a vase of flowers on a window sill, and with aristocratic gallantry presented each of the girls with a rose, which they accepted as if they had never received a more beautiful gift. Isn't it strange how the presence of young and pretty girls can temporarily change the whole personality of an old man? Larry had suddenly become fifty years younger, and he was not sparing in his compliments to the young beauty before him. I knew there would be no stopping him now. He was always nice to people, for he claimed, that every crowd had a silver lining.

'Will I tell the girls about the time I did the three months in jail on account of a woman,' he asked me with a plea in his eyes. I knew the story well—it was one of his standard lies, but I had not the heart to take away from him his hour of glory.

'Do, Larry,' I said, 'they'll love it.'

'Well, girls,' he said, having wiped the froth of his moustache with the sleeve of his coat, 'it happened a long time ago when I was very young. I was mending kettles and pots at the time and I went to Cork one day to buy solder. I happened to be passin' a polis barracks when this peeler came out and asked me politely if I'd mind standing in an identification parade. I needn't tell ye peelers don't talk politely to the likes of me, but I didn't want to go against the law in a strange city so I said "yes" even though I didn't know what in the hell an identification parade was. He brought me into a big room where there was nine other fellows standing up against a wall. He put me standin' with them. Then in comes this lovely blonde with the finest pair I ever saw in me life, God bless them, a short little dress that barely covered you-know-what, and a backside that waddled and bounced like a plate of jelly on a Sunday. By God, but she was a real beauty. She walked slowly up and down the line of us twice and then she put her hand on my shoulder and said: "That's the man." All the others started to move off and I made to go with them but the peelers got a hold of me and said: "You're not going."

'"Why not?" I asked.

'"Well," one of them said, "the girl identified you as the man who raped her down the Boggy Road last night. You're being charged with raping her and having carnal knowledge of her against her will." Now I couldn't have been the man who raped her because I was in Macroom, twenty miles away, that night. But I had another look at her and I was so proud she picked me out from all the others that I pleaded guilty, and by God the judge gave me three months in Limerick jail.'

There were loud guffaws of laughter from several others who had collected around. Larry took a swig out of his pint, now in his element with a mixed and captive audience, and said: ''Tisn't the only time I got into trouble over a woman, you know. I was out shooting wan day when I was young and I saw a big ball in the sky comin' down towards me. 'Twas a balloon with a man and a woman in it, but shure at the time I didn't know what a balloon was and I thought 'twas anti-Christ himself that was coming' at me. So I took aim with the gun and let fly. I must have hit it because it began to come down and I could see the man and the woman shakin' their fists at me, and I could hear them cursin' and swearin' at me. When they got over me what do you think the bloody man did? 'Tis no word of a lie—he took out his you-know-what and piddled down on top of me. Then the woman lifted her clothes and gave me the same dose, and I declare to God, wet an' all as I was, I had to walk three miles to the parish church to go to confession to the canon.'

There was now loud bursts of laughter from the crowd and Larry with feigned anger turned on them and said: 'What the hell are ye laffin' at? Shure I had to go to confession after seein' the things I saw.' Someone in the crowd shouted: 'Did you take pleasure in it, Larry?' And this caused still more laughter. I knew Larry was settling down for a session and the crowd was getting bigger, so before it was too late we slipped away. As we were going out the door he was off on another story talking so rapidly as though he begrudged the time to finish what he had to say.

Six months later Larry's stories came to a sudden end. He died in the Poor House and a benevolent state buried him in a paupers grave.

Back in Derrynane we had a quick lunch on board *Dualla*, and the loveliness of the day seems to have tempted the boys into taking our two young visitors on a rowing trip, meandering around the sun-splashed harbour and exploring the secret creeks and inlets that beckoned mysteriously and invitingly from the shore. Together with Maxie I took a different direction and strolled up from the pier to visit Derrynane House which is now an O'Connell museum and, to the credit of all responsible, magnificently preserved and cared for. The narrow road is partly covered in by interlacing archways of whispering, exotic, trees. Primroses showed their little golden heads through the long grass. Every plant and flower was blowing in the wind and putting the colour of summer on the earth. Here and there a playful squirrel jumped from branch to branch and the whole scene was as graceful as the gentle smile of an elegant old lady. Derrynane House has a strange mysterious beauty all its own like the smell of old lavender, lingering from a bygone age. I wandered through its stately vaulted rooms, gazing idly at the sombre-toned ancestral portraits on the walls, the glass-cases with all their mementoes of the centuries dead and gone, the hospitable banqueting table where every great Irishman of the age dined and discussed and debated the one burning topic of the day: how to free the Irish peasant from the intolerable slavery imposed upon him by the oppressor. I have always believed that the spirit of the past lives on, that nothing great ever dies, and as I wandered through this illustrious old house I felt the presence of those gigantic heroes in every nook and corner. Dominating all was the vibrant personality of Daniel O'Connell himself. He was born near Cahirsiveen in 1775 and he came to live in Derrynane while still a child. In those days it was a boy's paradise. The mountains were alive with rabbits and hares, woodcock and pidgeon filled the spinneys, grouse and pheasant were plentiful on the open moors while the encircling seas teamed with fish of every kind. The young O'Connell, steeped in this world of nature, grew up among the simple peasants, spoke only the Irish language, sang their songs, heard stories from their rich heritage of folklore and learned to master the complications of their strange character and personality. Later on in life this was to stand him in good stead. They were to follow him in their millions because no other Irish leader understood them as well as O'Connell. He was taught by a local hedge-schoolmaster, and later, by what was then known as a pushing master. When he was sixteen he was smuggled abroad to complete his education at St Omer in France. The seeds of greatness can sometimes thrive in isolation, and like many great men O'Connell's childhood was lonely, too. Although he romped and frolicked and sported with other children, he was often found hidden away among the wild rocks and shores reading a book, or just listening in silent contemplation to the sound of the sea. Yet his reading was not to dominate his life. 'Others studied books,' remarked Lecky, 'O'Connell studied men.' This loneliness and isolation was to remain with him all his days. No Irish leader, before or since, was ever so adored and cheered by the Irish people, yet he had only one real friend, his beloved wife. All others were acquaintances. Back in Ireland many years later, he qualified as a barrister and set up practice in Dublin. But before long he was deeply involved in politics and in a few short years he found himself leader of the Irish people in their long hard struggle for independence. His Catholic Emancipation in 1829, the victory we hail most today, was largely froth. The worst of the penal laws had been whittled away in the early years of the nineteenth century, mainly the result of a deal made by the Irish bishops with the British government, when the bishops promised to abandon their traditional nationalism and advise the people to become loyal English subjects. Archbishop Troy, the Catholic Archbishop of Dublin was one of the leaders of this about face and played a major part in cementing the Act of Union with England.

Having won Emancipation O'Connell threw himself fully into the fight for a Repeal of this infamous Act and the winning of Home Rule for Ireland. He fought ceaselessly in the British House of Commons, in the courts, in the press and at monster meetings at which, at times, over 250,000 people attended, and became a giant dominating the entire political scene. The British ruling classes hated him with a hatred that was paranoid. 'How long shall such a wretch as this be tolerated among civilised people,' screeched the *London Times* and later, added more venom by publishing the following lines about O'Connell:

> *Scum condensed of Irish bog*
> *Ruffian, coward, demagogue*
> *Boundless liar, base detractor*
> *Nurse of murders, treasons factor*
> *Of Pope and priest the crouching slave*
> *While thy lips of freedom rave.*
> *Spout thy filth, effuse thy slime*
> *Slander is in thee no crime*
> *Who would sue a convict liar?*
> *Or a poltroon who would fine?*
> *Then grant the monster leave to roam*

Let him salver out his foam;
Only give him length of string;
He'll contrive himself to swing.

The British government tried their best to buy him off and thereby end his political career. A chief justiceship became vacant and they offered it to him. O'Connell was constantly worried by shortage of money and debts, and this offer was very tempting. In terms of salary it would have meant the equivalent of £75,000 per annum in today's money. As well, he would only be required to work eighty days in the year and could spend the rest of his time living the life of a gentleman of leisure at Derrynane. It might be no harm to pause here and ask ourselves how many of us would turn down an offer like this? But O'Connell's soul was not for sale. He would have loved the job, and it would have meant an end to all his worries and troubles. How very very human was his comment: 'My heart is sad that I cannot take this job. I should enjoy the office exceedingly on every account if I could accept it consistently with the interests of Ireland—but I cannot.' Having failed with this ploy they tried another—the old favourite of emotional discredit which the British Foreign Office were to try so often again; on Parnell, Casement, De Valera, and Michael Collins. They paid one Eleanor Courtenay to write and publish a pamphlet stating that O'Connell raped her and was the father of her child, and that he had done the same to twelve other women. But her hysterical charge did not stick and few people, with the exception of the *London Times* believed it. Every one who was close to O'Connell knew of his deep love for his wife, Mary, and despite many searches there is nowhere a shred of evidence to show that he was the playboy the British Foreign Office tried to make him out to be. But Repeal never came and Irish Home Rule was as far away as ever. It is said that, however embarrassing to the government O'Connell's activities were, they could feel quite safe since he had an almost insane dislike for violence, and an equally insane trust in British politicians, especially if they had a title. They believed he was a bark without a bite, a sheep in sheep's clothing. With those two trump cards in their hands they could continually ignore him. Indeed towards the end they felt secure enough to clap him in jail. In 1847 worn, weary, exhausted and dying, he made one last appeal for the hundreds of thousands of Irish starving to death during the famine. Across the floor of the House of Commons he pleads with begging outstretched arms:

'Ireland is in your hands. She is in your power. If you do not save her she cannot save herself... a quarter of her population will perish unless you come to her relief.'

These were the last words of a dying man to the British Cabinet smugly seated opposite him. But these judicial murderers ignored him and sent, not a quarter of Ireland's population but over one half, to their deaths. O'Connell wanted to return to Derrynane but his doctors advised him to take to a warmer climate for a long rest. He set out for Rome but at Genoa could go no further. For nearly a week he lay in a coma, broken only by delirious attacks of defiance across the floor of the House of Commons. Later on that glorious May evening he turned to an aide and spoke: 'My dear friend, I am dying.' With these gentle words one of the greatest of Irish captains passed through the portals of this world and came face to face with his Maker.

When I left the house I went for a stroll through the old gardens and the pleasant shady walks which lie between the buildings and the wild sheltered valley. There was poetry in the well-kept lawns, where the daisies twinkled with delight and the butterflies danced as if they were puppets on invisible strings. The air was soft and sweet and the perfume of the richly coloured flowers mingled with the tender evening breeze. The sun was pouring its magic beauty through the openings in the trees and yet in the rapturous loveliness of this delightful summer's day I felt that sharp pain, which is given by the memory of something sweet that has vanished forever, and these strange little shivers of loneliness which sometimes come over a sorrowful heart:

But where are the loves of long ago?
O little twilight ship blown up the tide,
Where are the faces laughing in the glow
Of morning years, the last ones scattered wide?
Give me your hand, O brother, let us go
Crying about the dark for those who died.

As I rambled through the beautiful woodland paths I could hear the voice of silence speaking all around me. The dreamy hum of insects filled the air. The crimson bells of the fuschia were drooping their heads as if waiting for the bees. The trees threw soft shadows on the earth. On the path I found a dead robin and as I gently buried the little creature under a cluster of decaying leaves I remembered the words of a poem written for another dead robin long ago:

Tread lightly here, 'tis said,
When piping winds are hushed around,
A small voice wakes from underground,
Where now his tiny bones are laid.
No more in lone and leafless groves
With ruffled wing and faded breast,
His friendless, homeless, spirit roves;
Gone to the world where birds are blest;
Where never cat glides o'er the green,
Or school-boy's giant form is seen;
But love, and joy and smiling Spring
Inspire their little souls to sing.

I spent the next few hours meandering around the neighbourhood of Derrynane House, living in the past, almost hearing the voices of generations long since dead, strolling through the woodland paths, known only to last year's dying leaves, listening at times to the song of a blackbird drying its wings, sometimes resting in a shady tranquil corner, sometimes playing with Maxie as he chased the butterflies and insects from plant to plant and shrub to shrub, just drifting along like an empty bottle on an ebb tide. I strolled over towards Altar Hill from where I enjoyed a breathtaking view of the whole wild domain, and back again along a nature trail through a wild life sanctuary. I walked along the cool-ribbed sands, Maxie away ahead of me, with only the company of my long shadow in the evening sun. I crossed the rock to Abbey Island and visited the age-old graveyard, which is gradually being eaten away by the thunder blows of the constantly beating sea. Here in this beautiful spot lie the mortal remains of the great Kerry families, the O'Connells, the Galvins, the O'Sheas, the poet Tomas Rua O'Sullivan, as well as the unknown poor.

> *The boast of heraldry, the pomp of power*
> *And all that beauty, all that wealth e're gave*
> *Awaits alike the inevitable hour*
> *The paths of glory lead but to the grave.*

I lay down on the grass in the shadow of the ruined church overlooking the shore and watched the tumbling waves beating against the rocks. Far away overhead the sun-rimmed clouds flew by like sombre shadows between earth and heaven. A state of pleasant drowsy languor crept over me and I closed my eyes. I am not particularly psychic and I believe that the world we live in has enough of the marvellous and the mysterious to obviate the necessity of ventures into the supernatural, but there have been times in my life when, in one way or another, I felt a tangible contact with the past. I particularly recall one day I was climing Mount Brandon from the east face, and with each step I took, shivers of terror raced through my whole body. I felt the presence of some dreadful impending evil all around me. Reluctantly, I kept my silence and continued on until my companion turned to me and shouted almost hysterically: 'For Christ's sake let us go back. This bloody place smells of brimstone and hell.' As we took the path homeward together the sense of catastrophe lessened and lessened until it finally vanished near the foot of the mountain. But things were different today. I felt a happy and peaceful presence all around me as I wandered through the woodlands, and along the rocky shore, and I had no desire to run away. Most of the time my mind was occupied with thoughts on the great O'Connell, on the leadership of peoples and nations, and on the sad fact that this giant of

Irish politics failed so pathetically and so hopelessly. These perplexing thoughts were still in my mind as I lay back on the grass and as the sounds of the sea and of the land slowly faded into infinity.

Then it seemed to me as if I were suddenly possessed of a strange and new vision. The present slowly dissolved and the past came alive. Strange looking ships were anchored in the bay. Along the shore I saw groups of men dressed in unfamiliar clothes, attending to their nets. Children, also strangely dressed, were playing around the pools and rocks, their mothers sitting on the strand gossiping and embroidering. It was then I saw a tall regal figure coming towards me, with a large white cravat, long sweeping cloak, and head of dark luxurious hair tossing in the wind. I recognised him at once but I was in no way afraid. His kind open face spoke only of friendship and benevolence. He sat down on the grass to one side of me, took out a silver snuff-box from his vest pocket and smilingly offered me a pinch.

'You have been wondering why I failed,' he asked in a quiet voice. 'But I thought that should have been clear to every student of history who took the trouble to study my character.'

'It is not clear to me, at least,' I answered. 'You had Ireland in your hands like no leader ever before or since.'

'It is really quite simple,' he replied, taking another pinch of snuff. 'The fault lay not in my stars but in myself. I came to grief for three reasons. Firstly, I failed to grasp a simple but fundamental truth: *the British yield only to violence*. I thought I could bring about a revolution in Ireland through the democratic process but you cannot have a democracy without democrats. Brutality and tyranny were the weapons the British used against my peaceful overtures, and of course, I should have answered them with similar ones. But you see, violence was something that horrified me. I had seen the blood-stained streets of Paris and this left a deep and lasting impression on my young immature mind. But I realised, too late, if a man is trusted with the leadership of a great people he must put aside his personal feelings and do what he has to do. The well-meaning, but stupid, Home Rulers had to learn this bitter lesson too. It was only when Sinn Fein put its military wing, the IRA, into action that Ireland won freedom after a four year bloody struggle. The Home Rulers with their speech-making and pleading would never have got anything. If, instead of believing in non-violence, I had organised an efficient military wing, trained by French officers who were more than willing to come to our aid, I could have freed Ireland in a few years. If we had fought an all-out war against England then, several thousand lives might have been lost, but we would have had a free country by 1815, and there would have been no famine. Yes, perhaps ten thousand lives could have been lost, but I would have saved four million. Such are the vicissitudes of history. He who has the best battalions comes out on top, and this is all so sad.' He paused and looked reflectively out to sea for a few moments. Then he continued: 'The second great factor in my failure was that *I did my best to smash the Irish language*. I myself spoke Irish and French better than English. Practically all the audiences whom I addressed in Ireland spoke only Irish, yet to my eternal shame I spoke only English to them. This was unforgivable. I failed to recognise that a nation can never be a nation without its language. A nation cannot be economically sound and prosperous without its language—it becomes like an electric cable without electricity, an engine with the wrong fuel, a castrated bull. Other nations found this out and revived their languages when everything seemed completely shattered and broken—Czechoslovakia, Hungary, Romania, Bulgaria, Greece, Finland, and Israel. They all succeeded—only Ireland failed. Like those countries, we could have revived our language too when we got our freedom. The English used every form of brutality to crush the Irish language and turn the nation into a nation of cultural cretins, and I was one of those Irish leaders—indeed the principal one—who helped them.' He paused for a moment to take more snuff, and with slow careful deliberation closed his silver box and returned it to his vest pocket. He flicked a little dust off the edges of his coat and continued: 'The third great reason for my failure was that *I trusted the British Ruling Classes.* This was fatal. The average Englishman whom we deal with in the course of business, or whom we meet on holidays in Ireland, is usually a man of integrity who can be trusted and depended upon. But not so those involved in power politics. Irrespective of whether they were aristocratic, ecclesiastical, or commoners, treachery seemed to be their middle name. The knife was always at the ready to stick it in your back, and as they plunged it to the hilt they usually invoked the favour of Almighty God. Among the nations of the earth their rulers are the most untrustworthy. The ordinary citizen is as decent and honourable as one could ask to meet. I think the low-water mark of my career was when I knelt down to welcome King George to Dublin. This must have been the greatest act of toadyism in the history of the country. Others before me knelt to English monarchs but they did so with their tongues in their cheek. I was sincere because I stupidly thought that by giving my loyalty and trust I could win some goodwill for the starving Irish peasant. But I was mistaken. That imbecile was immune to any feeling of pity and humanitarianism, and he treated me and the Irish people like dirt. The scales fell from my eyes too late. So there you have it. There are the reasons why I think I failed and maybe in a hundred years time other leaders, if asked, would give the same reasons. We Irish never seem to learn from history. We keep making the same mistakes over and over again.'

He raised himself off the grass, looked at his watch and stood up.

'Do you think there is any hope for us as a nation?' I asked, 'or are we totally finished as a people?'

He gazed out to sea as if he were looking away beyond the horizon, away into the infinitude of space and time.

'At first sight,' he said reflectively, 'it looks hopeless. Ireland at the moment is going through a phase of plastic culture. Dublin, our capital, has more than its share of plastic men, in politics, in the professions, in business. The next time you are in Dublin take a good look at them in one of the fashionable eating places. They have plastic faces, plastic hair styles and plastic clothes. The chief characteristic of these blockheads is an expertise in being toadies. They discuss British books, not because they like them, but because they have inherited an age-old instinct to raise their forelock in the presence of what seems to be their betters. They go into ecstasies over modern art without having a clue as to what art is and could not tell the difference between a painting by Rembrandt and a cartoon of Micky Mouse. Most of them like to profess to be atheists, though not through conviction, but through stupidity. Their conversation can rarely rise higher than cheap compliments and a re-hash of the daily newspapers. But a great city like Dublin will survive all that, as it has survived other fads in the past.'

The old master of invective was running true to form. He who lacerated Biddy Moriarty, Ireland's most abusive fishwoman, and called Disraeli the last descendant of the unrepentant thief, had lost none of his touch.

'But all this is only the scum on the surface—and a real scum it is,' he continued. 'The young people today have seen through this empty shallow spuriousness and are rejecting it daily. You know yourself that never before in the history of the country was there such a great demand for Irish books. These young rising Irish have turned to their own literature, art, history and are spurning the counterfeits of this generation. Just look at the heights to which Irish music has jumped. Every concert hall that puts on a good show is packed. It is now virtually impossible to get a bed in any town where a *Fleadh Ceoil* is being held. If the Irish nation were dead the literature and music would be dead, too. But it is not. It was never more alive. It may be that some day a great Irish leader will arise, who will lead the nation, not only to cultural maturity but to economic and political maturity as well. A politician must live up to the highest standards he knows, not the lowest. Today's lies may well be tomorrow's truths. You are living in a great and exciting age and I only wish I could be part of it too.'

As he spoke these last words there was a distinct note of sadness .. his voice and a strange mist seemed to creep over his eyes. As he moved slowly away from me mumbling the words, 'great age... great age...', he seemed to have suddenly become older and more feeble, and as he picked his way across the sand dunes he was staggering rather than walking, an old broken man, symbol of the nation he left behind him. Soon his shattered frame was lost in the wild and desolate woods of Derrynane, and with him dissolved the scene before me.

Suddenly I heard a loud cracking noise. I opened my eyes and was wide awake. I had been asleep for nearly an hour. To my horror, as if to raise the whole scene to the heights of the macabre, Maxie appeared from nowhere with a human skull in his mouth. He resisted strongly, growled and protested vigorously as I removed it from between his paws. Who was it? What story could that lipless mouth tell? Where was its owner now? I placed it as reverently as I could in a niche high up on the wall of the ruined old church, away from the reach of marauding dogs. It matters not now who it was, rich or poor, high or low, man or woman. Death is the great leveller of all things. After a few months in the grave the lord looks exactly like the pauper. The fairness of God is infinite. His lark sings just as sweetly over the poorhouse as over the palace.

> *Imperious Caesar dead and turned to clay*
> *Might stop a hole to keep the wind away*
> *Oh that this dust which kept the world in awe*
> *Should patch a wall to stop the winter's flaw.*

3

For the man at sea in a small boat one of the most wonderful sounds is the lilting music of a soft breeze blowing through the rigging on a summer morning. It is a music that sweeps your thoughts out to sea, that pleads with you to arise and dress and leave behind the jaded weary land. It was this persuasive music that rang in my ears the next morning, and so, as the warm sunlight poured its refreshing rays into the cabin, I dressed, jumped into the punt and rowed ashore to give Maxie a run while the two boys got the breakfast. Less than half-an-hour later, when I returned, they had the main up and *Dualla* ready to sail, and in a few moments the anchor was free and we glided out through the narrow entrance into the wide open sea. Our plan was to take a trip up one side of Kenmare Bay and down the other and then spend the night in the lea of Horse Island in Ballinskelligs Bay. A fresh and gentle south west wind blew like a happy sigh over the water, filled *Dualla's* sails and sent her dancing over the shimmering waves. We sat out on deck, having our breakfast in the most glorious surroundings imaginable. When we turned the corner at Lamb's Head the whole beautiful panorama of Kenmare Bay opened up before us. Little roads and winding paths climbed through the folds of the Kerry mountains as they rose serenely from the picturesque shoreline. The blue-grey tops of the boulders, tinted with golden whin, gave a touch of fairyland to the distant landscape. July was covering up the greens of June, with flowers, and blooms, and purple heather.

> *Ba thaitneamhach aoibhin suiomh na sléibhte*
> *Ag bagairt a ginn thar dhroim a chéile*
> *Do ghealfadh an croí a bhí crión le cianta*
> *Caite gan bhrí no liónta i bpianta...*

It was the kind of day one likes to remember in the depth of winter. We were, all three of us, filled with the joy of the moment, relaxing to the movement of the heaving, restless sea. One of the delightful things about the sea is its constantly changing moods. There are times when it radiates a heavenly blue that speaks of young love and the thousand promises of happiness life holds out in those days of innocent hope. Other times it is dull grey-green, gloomy and desolate, reflecting the harsh reality, that not even one of those beckoning promises of youth is ever fulfilled. Again the sea can be almost crystal clear and you can spend a happy hour or two peering over the side of a boat at a whole new world of marine life beneath the surface. But it is when the sea is in a savage mood that it is at its most awe-inspiring. When the great battles between wind and wave take place, and the whole force of the Atlantic Ocean crashes against the shores of Kerry, spray and spume, and even rocks, are hurled violently into the air and onto the land. Lighthouse doors have been smashed, and freak waves of enormous height have shattered the lanterns themselves. Indeed it can be quite dangerous to drive in a car along the road around Slea Head in a bad south west gale, for it has been known that showers of rocks and stones have been tossed high into the air and on to the road by the power of the waves. Kruger Kavanagh, God rest him, was once going to Dingle with a creel, in which he had a goat in heat, that he was bringing for service to a puck. There was a fierce south west gale blowing and when they got beyond Slea Head Kruger heard terrible screeching and milemurder behind him. When he looked around what did he see but a six foot conger eel which had been flung up by an enormous wave, and had landed right into the creel. According to Kruger, the cause of all the commotion was, that the conger sensed the goat was in heat, and wanted to have a bit of fun himself, but the goat wasn't too keen, seeing that she had never seen a puck with two blue eyes, a smile, and several wobbly fins. Kruger had to call on a couple of road-workers for help and it took three strong men to pull the conger off the unwilling goat. Howsoever, *biodh sin mar ata*, Atlantic storms are best watched from a safe offing on the land. Two or three times in my life I have been caught out on *Dualla* in violent gales and not only do I never want to repeat the experience, but I do not even want to think about them. And yet everything in life has its place. Were it not for these Atlantic storms our shores would be as uninteresting as the banks of a canal. The raging seas wear down the rocky coasts and chisel out myriads of varying shapes and forms that give a wild and rugged beauty, to fill the heart with gladness or sorrow, to inspire the poet to write, the artist to paint, and the young lover to dance upon a star. Have you ever noticed that people who live close to the sea are moulded and formed by the richness of its moods? These thoughts crossed my mind as we sailed this beautiful coastline, listening to the sound of the waves rippling along *Dualla's* sides like the laughter of young girls, gazing at the blue-brown rocks of the shore, bathed in the heaving summer sea. What else but the surging sea could have given Kerry people such remarkable versatility? They are poets, artists, writers, storytellers, saints and sinners. A Kerry peasant is a far more cultured man than the boring, empty, self-opinionated intellectual who may have some brains but little intelligence. Anew MacMaster once said that he would far prefer to perform *Hamlet* or *Macbeth* before an audience of Kerrymen who could not speak a word of English than in the most sophisticated city auditorium. But for all their great artistic qualities they are very human, shrewd, loveable, with a moderate touch of deviousness.

There was an old Kerry farmer one time, who was a Protestant, and when he was drawing close to ninety years of age he called to see the canon one cold winter's night, and told him that he wanted to become a Catholic and be baptised in that church. Naturally the canon was delighted —this was the first convert he ever had—and it called for a celebration, not just ordinary whiskey, but a little drop of the poteen, which the canon had in hide since he got it the previous Lent from a reformed drunkard, who was going on the dry for the holy season, and who in a moment of religious fervour presented his unused stock to the priest. When the old farmer and the canon had toasted each other a few times the canon inquired as to the reason why such a staunch Protestant would want to change his religion at that late hour of his life.

'Tell me, Sam,' he asked, 'was it the good Christian example of your Catholic neighbours that moved you to join our Holy Mother Church?'

'Well, not exactly that, Canon,' answered Sam. 'You know yourself that the graveyard in this parish is divided into two sections, one for Protestants, and the other for Catholics, separated by a row of palm trees. Well, for the last seventy years I have been attending the funerals of my Catholic neighbours and the same thing happens every time: we all gather in the pub and have a few drinks, and when the hearse arrives we then move into the graveyard across the road, to say a few prayers and pay our respects. Then when all is over, and the corpse well buried, every man in the graveyard that's half full of porter, crosses over through the trees and relieves himself on the Protestant graves. Now, Canon, I want to be a Catholic so that I can be buried in the Catholic section for I have no mind to be put down where the farmers of the county will be pissing on top of me until the Last Day.' And the canon, being a sensible man and a farmer's son himself, understood, so they filled their glasses once more and drank a toast to the One, True, Holy and Catholic Church. Sam was well thought of in the whole Kingdom of Kerry. He was hard working and industrious. He started in a small way and ended up a man of substance and means, that any bank manager would be delighted to shake hands with. He got his start in life through a well-to-do Protestant woman, a little older than himself, who lived in the parish and whose husband died suddenly and left her childless, but with a large well-stocked farm. Sam knew them fairly well, so a few weeks after the funeral he called down one Sunday night to see the widow and to sympathise with her. They had a great chat by the fire and when Sam was going home he left the lid of his pipe after him, in a little cubbyhole over the hon. That meant, of course, that he had to come back the following Sunday night to get the lid. Himself and the widow had another great chat that night and when Sam was going home he left a cut of tobacco after him, so he had to come back the next Sunday to collect it. This went on for four or five weeks, him forgetting something every time with the widow getting fonder and fonder of him every day. In the end before anyone knew about it the two of them slipped off to Cork and got married in the cathedral. This was the beginning of Sam's good fortune and from that day forward he never looked back and he died a good Catholic.

We sailed along up the coast keeping well out from this beautiful seaboard in order to avoid a few dangerous rocks on the way: Brigbeg, a sunken rock near Illaunaweelaun, the Beara Rocks near West Cove, where incidentally there is a delightful and safe anchorage, Carrigheela Rock guarding the entrance to Castle Cove. All these rocks cover at high water and can be quite dangerous if one is tempted to approach the shore too closely. The whole poetic landscape along this coast is rooted in the past and exudes a silence that seems to be older than the earth. Every valley is immersed in the sadness of history, for it was all along here that some of the worst atrocities in the blood-stained history of Ireland took place. Folk tradition in these rural places tells of a Cromwellian sadist named Captain Barrington, who kept a highly trained blood-hound to amuse him by tearing women and children apart. His particular pleasure was to watch the hound rip unborn infants from pregnant women. But once, when it was savaging a seven year old child in front of its parents, a young Irishman named Brennan from nearby Ballycarnahan attacked the animal with his bare fists and tore its jaws apart. For this there was a price put on his head and he had to go on the run. Barrington was in charge of a company of English soldiery whose brutalities are still talked of around Kerry firesides.

They tell how this company slaughtered blind and feeble men, women, boys and girls, idiots and old people, and how when all resistance was at an end, these soldiers forced the people into old barns which they then set on fire, putting to the sword any who tried to escape; how soldiers were seen to catch up screaming children on the points of their swords, making them squirm in the air in their death agony; or yet again how women were found hanged from trees, with their children at their bosoms strangled in the hair of their mothers. Sadly enough Captain Barrington was the rule, not the exception, and it is conservatively estimated that more than one million Irish men, women and children, out of a total population of one and a half million met their deaths in this way.

We had now reached the entrance to Sneem harbour and were sailing between Sherky Island and Pidgeon Island on our way to the little bight north east of Garnish where we had planned to anchor and lunch. Sherky Island has always been a bit of a mystery to me. In Irish it is *Inis na Searcha*, which translated means the Island of Love, and I have wondered a great deal how it came to have a name like that, but my two young companions had no doubts whatever. It was a quiet remote place, they said, where, in the dim and distant past the clergy could slip across for a frivolous weekend without giving scandal to any of their flock, or alternatively it could be on such an island that the local chieftain enjoyed the fruits of his *ius noctis* claim. I doubt if the answer to the problem is quite as simple as that, but they had a point, in so far as the attitude of the ancient Irish to sex was very matter-of-fact and magnanimous. Indeed the old Brehon laws, which were in force up to the twelfth century, had a far more sensible approach to sexual misdemeanours than we have today. There is very little reference to pre-marital sex, so it seems as if it were taken as a matter of course; the emphasis was on much more serious aspects, such as castration, rape and divorce. For example if a man had his penis cut off by a jealous rival he was entitled to two forms of compensation; he could demand that the same be done to the perpetrator, and he could also claim one third of his property. If, on the other hand, his scrotum were cut off, for some strange reason he would be entitled only to property compensation. Rape is dealt with on the basis of whether it is violent or not, and in one subsection there is the rather severe death penalty for a man who, before or after raping a woman, shaves off her pubic hair and makes fun of her for the amusement of his friends. Divorce was much easier for a woman than for a man. She could divorce him if he insulted her in public, struck her so as to leave a mark, refused to have intercourse with her, preferred the company of servant boys, or indeed refused to give her whatever food or delicacies she required. So with this fairly healthy outlook on sexual matters there are all kinds of activities that could cause an island to be called an Island of Love. However, we sailed quite close but we could see no evidence of anyone besporting themselves in the aforesaid manner, and when we had cleared the rocks off the northern corner of the small Inish Keragh we lowered our sails and motored in to anchor off Garnish, in an anchorage so breathtakingly beautiful that it could truly be called paradise. There was one other yacht in the little bay, which I took to be English because she was flying the red ensign, and no sooner had we anchored than the owner hailed and invited us over for a drink. The boys decided to stay on board *Dualla* to get lunch ready, so I got into the punt and rowed across, promising faithfully to be back in half-an-hour. I kept my promise, but this I must say: it was one of the most enlightening and revealing half hours of my life.

The owner was from the North of Ireland and I suppose he could be technically called British. His companions had gone up the estuary in their punt to buy groceries and other supplies in Sneem. When I pointed out to him as diplomatically as I could, that it might not be too safe for an Ulster yacht to fly a British flag in Cork or Kerry he seemed a trifle taken aback.

'I never really thought about this,' he said. 'But now that

you mention it I can see your point. All round it would probably be safer for us to keep a low profile in Southern waters.'

When the drinks were poured I casually remarked, in a rather conventional way, that I hoped all this trouble in the North would be over soon and that everyone could not only sail in peace but live in peace.

'I don't think it's going to be all that easy to end matters,' he said. 'I am convinced that it will go on for a long long time yet.'

'Surely a little good will on both sides could help,' I answered. 'After all we are rational human beings and if people of different cultures, languages and religion can live in harmony in Switzerland, surely it ought to be possible for us to do the same on this small island.'

'You know,' he said, 'I come South a lot. I love cruising in Southern waters. I meet quite a number of other yachtsmen like yourself and we talk openly and freely about this matter. But I must say that I find here in the Republic a gross misunderstanding of the real issues involved.'

'But is the issue not basically a religious one?' I asked. 'And surely everyone in the North must realise that in this day and age, the Catholic Church in the South is politically a spent force. Hardly anyone now pays the slightest attention to the pronouncements of the bishops—their power and influence are at an end. They over-reached themselves in the past and they no longer hold the confidence of the people.'

'Yes, I think that's fairly generally recognised,' he said, 'but the issue is *not* a religious one—let me emphasise that. The issue is purely an *economic* one. That is what you don't understand in the South. Let me try to explain more clearly. I am a Protestant Unionist, but I don't really care a fig about the Protestant religion, nor do I care a rattling damn about the Queen or the Union Jack. I am not loyal to any of these things—I am loyal to myself and my class. My ancestors took the lands by force from the Irish a few hundred years ago, and by God we intend to keep them. We planters have had all the goodies, all the plum jobs, all the power, all the influence, and as long as we stay with Britain that's how things are going to be. That's why we are Unionists. If by some miracle the Republic could guarantee us all the goodies, and if we could trust them, we would become Republicans in the morning. You in the South never seem to understand that our Protestantism, our Unionism, our loyalty to the Queen are only all so many red-herrings, so many catch-cries, to keep us in power and to ensure that we and our class get everything that's going. When partition was being brought about in 1922 the original plan was that all nine counties of Ulster would be separate from the South. But when we did our sums we found out that, if that were to be the case, the nationalists would be in a majority, so we promptly dropped the three counties to ensure that there would always be a Unionist government. Remember, we've had the goodies, we want them, and we're going to keep them.'

'But isn't it true,' I said, 'that over the past few years the Irish government have publicly committed themselves to a policy of ensuring that if the North were to come in the Protestants would get absolute fair play and every chance, and that religion and politics would be no barrier to advancement.'

'In the first place,' he replied, 'we don't want fair play. We want everything. In the second place we don't trust the two-faced Irish government. Every thinking person in the North knows that no Irish government since the inception of the state wants partition to end. Oh, yes. They have shouted the very opposite from every platform but the plain fact is that the ending of partition would spell doom for the major Irish political parties. Just consider for a moment what would happen if partition were ended. There would be approximately thirty extra seats in Dail Eireann to be filled, and with all the different groups and loyalties in the North, neither of the main Southern parties would get a look in, so that you would have an unpredictable thirty seats of Unionists, Labour, Alliance, Republicans and other splinter groups, who could cause havoc with the balance of power in Dail Eireann. It could mean the end of any party ever having an overall majority. One of your problems is you've never had a statesman in the South of the calibre of Adenauer, de Gaulle or Gaspari. De Valera was primarily a politician. He was not a statesman. He did not try to create a great Irish nation. He tried, and succeeded, to create a great political party. Since the inception of your state you have been led by politicians, who, being intelligently dishonest, were only concerned with power, and the ending of partition would mean the end of the almost absolute power which they now enjoy. No, my dear friend, the last thing an Irish government wants is for partition to end, but like us, who use the Queen and the Union Jack as red-herrings, you use partition and the Irish language. It's all part of the game of power, part of the struggle for the goodies. We in the North want partition to stay so that we can have our goodies. You in the South want partition to stay so that you can have your goodies. Idealism or love of country does not enter into it.'

'And so,' I mused, 'thousands of simple people must die or be maimed for life so that politicians on both sides of the border may have their absolute power.'

'Exactly,' he answered, 'you've put your finger on it.'

'But is there any hope at all?' I asked. 'Any silver lining in any cloud?'

'It's hard to say right now,' he answered thoughtfully. 'Speaking as a Unionist what we fear most is the Provisional IRA. They mean business. Their overall policy is to force the British withdrawal through violence, and in that they have summed up the position accurately. They know that all the lessons of history show that the British yield only to violence, and not to peaceful negotiations. It may well be that in time the British people will get fed up of pouring money and men into Northern Ireland, and withdraw. If that happens, and it is quite on the cards, then moderate Unionist opinion could very well accept the inevitable, and go for some form of federal union with the Republic as the lesser of two evils. As I told you before Unionists have loyalties only to themselves, and if they can made a deal with the Republic, where they can still have most of the goodies, they will do so. So as you can see it's all still in the melting pot. Anyway, it's a fine summer's day, so let's forget all this bloody politics and talk about something else. Tell me about your cruise.' And so we dropped the politics and chatted about cruising, harbours, pubs, boats, and all the stock-in-trade conversation of yachtsmen, until we saw in the distance his companions returning from Sneem with their supplies. I got into the punt to row back to *Dualla*, but before moving off I thanked him for the drink but above all for his honest, straight-forward and stimulating conversation.

'It was a pleasure to have you,' he replied with a smile. 'And thanks for the tip about the flag. There is an old proverb which says that discretion is the better part of valour, so I'll leave the valour to one side, and remove the flag this moment. My Unionism does not rise to the extent of having my yacht sunk.'

After lunch I brought Maxie ashore for a quick run and then we broke anchor and sailed out into the bay, leaving Sherky Island to starboard and Rossdrohan to port. We set course due south east for Kilmackilloge harbour, where unfortunately, we would not have time to anchor if we were to make Ballinskelligs before dark. It was high summer. The rugged Kerry hills which surrounded us on all sides were mixing their heather browns with the July greens. The rosy edged clouds wound their arms around the tops of the faraway mountains. There was a slight mist on the shore that made parts of the ground look like a lake, but it was a transparent elfish mist that gave a soft tenderness to the landscape. The gulls were sailing almost motionless in the sun-kissed air, and making strange muffled sounds as if they were murmuring the secrets of their hearts to each other. Here and there a dolphin jumped out of the water, which brought Maxie to the alert. Then there were several, all jumping and frolicking with the joy of being alive. It was a happy day.

As I gazed dreamily up into the Kerry hills I remembered one of those strange adventures that often befall a man when he is young and free from care. It happened during the war when I was stationed in Cork. De Valera, who was our Taoiseach at the time, had the reputation of never forgetting his old IRA comrades in arms, and when one of them died he made a special point of expressing his condolences. His enemies said that he divided funerals into three classes: 1. He attended in person if the funeral were likely to be a big one; 2. he sent a representative, usually an army officer, if the funeral were likely to be only of middling size, and 3. he just sent a telegram for funerals likely to be small. However true or false that speculation may be, I was detailed one fine summer's day, to represent him at the funeral of an old IRA man right in the heart of these Kerry hills. As the burial was taking place early in the morning I drove from Cork to Kenmare the evening before, so as to make sure I would be in time. The next day was a fair day in Kenmare and most hotels were full, but after a search I managed to get a bed in a room sharing with a cattle-drover. After supper I met my room companion and we adjourned to the bar together for a few drinks. He was a hardy looking man in his mid-fifties with a rugged rural face, a nose like a ferret and a head of grey hair plastered over a bald patch of uncertain cleanliness. He smelt of the country, the fields, the bogs and I liked him. His entire luggage consisted of an old trench-coat and an ash plant.

'I don't bother with a handy-bag,' he told me. 'I have to be at the fair at five o'clock in the morning and when the cattle are sold I hit the road away home for myself. Anyway if I had a handy-bag the tinkers might think 'twas full of money and maybe they'd beat me up and take all I had.'

We chatted over our drinks about fairs, cattle, pigs, politics, football, the war and when I told him I was going to a funeral the following day, and gave him the name of the dead man, he was able to give me precise directions. I was glad of that because I was completely confused by the variety of roads on the army map I had with me. He knew the family, he said, and he explained to me how to get to the graveyard. I recall that having passed an old ruin several miles out I was to go through a cross-roads, and then when I came to a thatched house I should turn left and the graveyard was only a few miles further on. As the night passed and we kept replenishing our drinks he became more and more talkative. He took out his pipe and cleaned it with a horse-nail, and finally launched out into his life story.

'I spent twenty-five years working for a farmer,' he said, 'and I can tell you if ever you work for a Kerry farmer you can be sure you'll see the sun rise every morning, and you'll be so tired when you sit down your two feet will think you are out of your mind. Well, this fellow I worked for was no great shakes. He was only a servant boy that married into a farm without a pound note in the heel of his fist—that was because nobody else would have her—you see she started off as a maid in a Big House and 'tis said that she lifted her skirt high and often for the squire, and when he got tired of her he settled her down on a farm of land. She was damaged goods, don't you see, and she found it hard to get a man with money. I can tell you that they were two of the meanest people I ever met in me life. She wouldn't give a halfpenny to a tramp even if she was flapping her wings on the way to heaven, and I saw him once giving a beggar woman a crust of bread as hard as the irons of hell, with two inches of grey scum on it so that you'd think 'twas baked in the year of the famine. He was a lazy divil too. You can be sure he never sweat enough to drown a flea. By the way, did you ever know that them that doesn't sweat, pisses twice as much as them that do. That's a fact and 'tis no laughing matter either. Anyway, I spent a great lot of me time when I was working for them, followin' a stallion. You see they had a stallion that used to service mares and I had to do all the dirty work. When the stallion would see a mare in the field he'd know that she wasn't brought there to bid him the time of day, and he'd go fair mad—'twould take the divil himself to hould him quiet. After a bit of prancing around the field the mare would quieten down, and start twisting her tail to one side in a rougish class of a way. And then when the stallion mounted her I'd have to direct his implement to the right target or otherwise we'd be in one hell of a pucker. Do you know I spent twenty-five years of me life at that game, and one fine day the thought crossed me mind that all the stallions I handled were having the best of fun and here was me, getting on in years, with no bit of fun at all. So I thought to meself that 'twas time for me to change things and to be able to look forward to a bit of drollery when I came home in the evening. So one Sunday after early Mass, I said to meself that a clocking hen never got fat, and I hit the road up to Lyreacrompane to Dan Paddy Andy, the matchmaker, to see if there was any chance he could find the likes of me a wife. When I got there he wasn't at home, for he had to bring his sow to a farmer that had a boar, and lived about a mile away, so I had to wait. I took a stroll for meself around a knobbly ould field that I'd say wasn't ploughed since the year of the flood, and after about half-an-hour Dan came back with the sow asleep in a wheelbarrow. He wheeled the animal into the haggard and upended her into the dung-heap and then we got down to business. When I told him what brought me he looked me up and down, and then looked closer at me head of grey hair. "Ah, well," he said, "there's manys the mountain with snow on the top and heat in the valley, and no matter how much speed the young goat has 'tis often the ould lame puck gets out the gap first. But when a man is as crabbed as you are he'd want to make sure that his machinery is well oiled and in good working order, for you can't put a hare out of a bush if there's no hare there." He took out a stump of a pencil, spat on it, and wrote something on a bit of a matchbox. "There's an address of an eatin' house in Tralee. Take a day or two off and go there. The woman of the house is a friend of mine and she'll look after you. You'll find out all you want to know about your machinery there, and if you still want a wife when you come back, call up some day and I'll be able to fix you.

And if I do get a wife for you don't spare her. You should never spare a wife or a jennet if you want to keep the bailiff away from your door." Well, anyway I did what he told me and when I got a chance I struck the road for Tralee and after a bit of a search I found the eatin' house. 'Twas late at night when I knocked at the door and I can tell you I got a bit of a fright when I saw the ould witch that let me in. She was a withered looking hag, with a long neck like a sick gander, and a pair of shanks that wouldn't make garters for a servant of Cromwell. She looked for all the world like as if she was kept in vinegar all her life. By God, I said to meself, if Dan Paddy Andy wants me to practise on her he has another think coming to him. However, fair play to her, she gave me a fine mug of tea and a feed of cold pig's head and then brought me up to my room. I can tell you I was the happy man when I saw the tail end of her skirt going down the stairs. No sooner was she gone than there was a knock on the door, and in walks this young one as bold as if she knew me all her life, hoppin' around the room like a pullet with fleas. There's no doubt about it but she was a fine looking heifer, with fingers like them small sausages you'd get at wakes. She had the best pair of you-know-what I ever saw and they were standin' up the same as if they was sprung. She was the cause of confession for me. She took off her blouse and sat down beside me on the bed, and said she came for what Dan Paddy Andy sent me for. Anyway we got down to business, but then she started to kick up a row because I wouldn't take off me britches. Don't you see I was afraid, for I had over £100 sewn into me back pocket that I was savin' up to buy a stallion of me own, and I was sure 'twould be stolen if I took them off. I couldn't tell her the real reason so I did a bit of quick thinking and told her I wouldn't like to take them off for 'twould be a mortal sin. You see I thought she was a religious class of a one, because the first thing she did when she came into the room was to turn the face of the Sacred Heart picture to the wall. But the bloody little bitch only burst out laughing in me face, and asked me was I sure I didn't want to say the Rosary before I started. However, we got to work and by God I can tell you she didn't come down with the last shower. The whole room went spinnin' around—'twas then I understood why 'twas so hard to hold back a stallion—and I can tell you that Dan Paddy Andy needn't have any fears about the heat of the valley or the hare in the bush and when 'twas all over she reached out her hand to her bag and produced a noggin of whisky. I took several swigs and I never felt better. I don't know whether she was coddin' me or not when she asked me would I like to sing *Faith of our Fathers*, but I didn't mind for I felt so good that I wouldn't call the Queen me aunt. We lay down on the bed side by side, me with me arm around her and she ticklin' the tip of her nose on the hair in me ears. I don't remember no more till I woke up late next mornin' with a splittin' headache and a mouth like the inside of a hen-house. The one was gone, and so was me £100, ripped out of me back pocket. I jumped into me clothes and ran downstairs and I fairly attacked the ould hag in the kitchen. Instead of having any understanding for me she abused me like a dog. She had thunder and lightning in her eyes and her tongue cut the ground from under me. She kept a decent house, she said, and if I thought fit to bring a tally-woman up to my room she knew nothing about it and wouldn't stand for it. She shouted out the back for someone to come out and go for the guards, for jail was too good for the likes of me. When she mentioned the guards I took to me heels out the door and away with me down the street and she still shoutin' abuse after me. I don't rightly know what happened to me after that. Everything went sort of queer in me head. I was twenty-five years savin' that £100 and now 'twas gone. It seems as if I walked out the Cork road talkin' loud to meself, and then I have a memory of men in uniform puttin' me into a van. Anyway, to make a long story short, I came to in the mental home in Killarney, in a room full of lunatics. They kept me there for three months before I got right in the head again, and then they let me go. I never went back to the farmer and I had enough of bloody stallions — 'twas they caused all the trouble. I took up cattle-drovin' and I'm at it ever since. And I can tell you this—I'm not one bit sorry, for I made a handy pile of money at it, so that I often say to meself that it might be all for the good.'

'Did you never think of going back to Dan Paddy Andy and trying for another woman,' I asked, 'after all, you found out that everything was in order.'

'Ah the curse of hell on that blackguard,' he answered. 'I wouldn't trust him no more. You'd never know what kind of cross-eyed heifer he'd spancel me up with. No, I'll stay on me own now. An empty house is better than a bad lodger. I'm too old now anyway. There's no use tryin' to draw Christian blood from a tinker's nose. Anyway, I'd have nothing to do with women no more, and you're a young man now and I'd give you the same advice and you put it in your pocket or under the bed, whatever you like.' It was closing time. 'Have one last drink,' he said. ''Tisn't always the money is rattling in me pocket.' We had a quick drink and wound our unsteady way up the stairs to bed. I fell into a deep sleep and remembered nothing until the bright morning sun came shining in the windows.

When I awoke my friend was gone and I presumed he was at the fair, so shortly after breakfast I drove out into the country to find the cemetery where the funeral was taking place. After a few false turns I finally found the old ruin, described by the drover, and after that the cross-roads and the thatched house, and a little further on the graveyard. A large crowd had collected around the open grave, where the priest was saying aloud those beautiful and inspiring prayers of hope from the liturgy for the dead. I waited discreetly on the outskirts until the grave was filled in, and then quietly made my way towards the bereaved widow. She seemed somewhat surprised and puzzled to see me as if a man in uniform were out of place at her husband's funeral. I introduced myself and explained that Mr De Valera had sent me to represent him and to express his condolences. At this she burst out crying, took my hand between hers and asked me to tell Mr De Valera how much the family appreciated his noble gesture. 'And,' she added, 'never in our lives have one of us voted or supported Mr De Valera. You can also tell him that from this day forward every relative we can find will support him and vote for his party in every election.'

Sometimes in the confusion of crowds one does not think too clearly and it was only as I was leaving the graveyard I had the feeling that something was not quite right. First of all the widow was, at most, in her late twenties, which seemed rather young for the widow of an old IRA man. Again, there was no tricolour on the coffin. Could Mr De Valera have made a mistake? The priest who had said the prayers was just about to move off in his car when I hailed him, introduced myself and told him my mission, and asked if everything were alright. He burst out laughing and then excused himself for laughing at a funeral.

'You see,' he said, 'this family have been bitterly anti-De Valera all their lives. You are at the wrong funeral. The old IRA man whose funeral you should be at, is being buried about six miles away. He bore the same surname as the man who was buried here today. Maybe that's how you mistook the event. If you hurry now you might catch the right funeral.' He gave me directions on how to get there, and I got into my car, roundly cursed the drunken cattle-drover, and drove as fast as I could to the right graveyard. When I got there the burial was over, the crowd gone, and only the grave-diggers left. I found the widow with her friends and relatives in the snug of a nearby public house. I explained who I was but before I had time to sympathise she stopped me angrily and said: 'We were told by the guards you were coming, and we held up the funeral for nearly an hour, but you never turned up. Go back now and tell Mr De Valera that never again will I or any of my family or relatives ever vote for, or support, himself or his party. He has insulted the memory of my late husband by sending his representative nearly two hours late.' I tried to mutter and apology but she sharply ordered me out of the house.

The following year the army was engaged on large scale summer manoeuvres, and Mr De Valera himself paid us a visit, and stayed with us most of one day. In the evening he was sitting on the grass chatting idly to four or five of us young officers, when in a moment of bravado I plucked up courage to tell him the story of the two funerals. He burst out laughing, and then called over Oscar Traynor, Minister for Defence, and made me repeat the story in full for him. Later as they were leaving De Valera, still chuckling, shook hands with me and said: 'The votes you lost at one funeral, you picked up at the other, so we cannot be too hard on you.'

Kilmakillogue is one of those enchanting, bewitching harbours that poets write about and artists never tire of painting. Its deep sheltered inlets are surrounded by hills and mountains of bright yellow gorse, purple heather and slate-blue boulders, while shadowy woods of whispering trees descend serenely to the water's edge. Here and there in the openings, small farmsteads dot the landscape, their little gardens of potato and corn gently sloping to the sea. And of course there is a graveyard, an old graveyard where

> ... *the faithful, with their arms upon their breast*
> *Hear no more the voice they loved so well.*

There are three excellent anchorages in Kilmakillogue, one on the south east near Dereen House, another south west of Bunaw Pier, and best of all Collorus, where I once spent three delightful days sheltering *Dualla* from a storm. There was hardly a ripple on the calm water while outside force eight winds sent the wild waves crashing in thunderous cascades the whole length of Kenmare Bay. During those few days I explored, in the punt, all the little inlets and creeks of Kilmakillogue, visiting Lauragh, where Renunccini's Dean, Marsari, was so well treated by the Irish peasants; Dereen gardens, with their towering ferns, long-limbed bamboos, exotic eucalyptus, and trees of mountain ash which keep away vampires and other such evil things; the ruins of Bunaw church from whence, in 690, the great St Killian left Ireland for Wurzburg and martyrdom. And although shops were few and far between, the little farmhouses generously sold me eggs, butter, milk, bread and bacon. Indeed, in many cases it was difficult to get them to accept payment at all.

But today we did not have enough time to anchor and do any exploring, so we just sailed in and around Spanish Island, out again, and back on our homeward journey down the centre of Kenmare Bay. We chatted, talked, told stories, sang songs, made tea and hardly felt the hours passing until, late in the evening, when the golden sun was dropping off the edge of the horizon, we sailed between Scariff and Deenish and dropped anchor in the lea of Horse Island in Ballinskelligs Bay. This is a good anchorage, but it has the drawback of being a long row from the pier, and a still longer walk to the village. The boys brought Maxie for a run on the island, and by the time we had had our dinner over it was already dark, and much too late to go ashore, so for a short while we listened to light music on the radio and then went to bed.

4

We were up and about early in the morning because we had made up our minds to move on to Valentia and take in the Skellig Rocks. We calculated this would occupy the best part of the day and leave no time to visit Waterville, a delightful village and the only place I know where that rare delicacy, farmer's salty butter, can be purchased. Not far up the road from the pier are the ruins of the intriguing Ballinskelligs Monastery where one John O'Mulchonry was abbot, but he was removed from office because a Bantry man,

Dermot O'Sullivan, alleged that he was 'an open and notorious fornicator and converted the goods and monies of the monastery to his own use.' There seems to have been some substance for these charges because, although he was sacked, he managed to pull enough strings to get one of his sons elected abbot in his stead.

It was a delightful summer's morning as we upped anchor and made sail. The wind was slightly over force three blowing from a point west of south, so we hoisted a medium foresail on the principle that it is easier to change up in light winds than down in stormy winds, and set our course for the Skellig Rocks, those bleak islands with sides like steel. As we cleared the turbulent seas around Bolus Head I remembered that it was here, nearly 4000 years ago, the Milesians landed to make a home in Ireland. They brought with them a poet called Amergin who was so moved by the beauty of the Kerry coast that he wrote a delightful poem which is still recited today:

I am the air that kisses the waves,
I am the wave of the deep,
I am the whisper of the surf,
I am the eagle on the cliff,
I am a ray from the pure sun,
I am the grace of growing things,
I am a lake in the rolling meadows,
Who if not I?

As we sailed out into the deep blue sea, and with Amergin's poem in my mind, I slipped the moorings of material things and went rambling along the byways of thought. In those far-off days, Amergin, a pagan, and with the true insight of a poet, experienced the existence of a very real God. His God was so far removed from the strange God that I, and hundreds of thousands of other Irish children like me, were taught to believe in in the impressionable years of our youth. To us God was an old man, with a beard like Brian Boru, sitting up on a remote throne surrounded by angels playing harps. He was a severe man of justice, who had an endless army of clerks counting up all our failings, even *every idle word that men shall speak*, all our little sins, and for these he would meet out the most terrible punishment. Quite recently I came across a copy of the Catechism which I had to learn off by heart under pain of a severe hiding from my teacher. It makes strange reading today. This Catechism reminded me how depraved I was because Adam and Eve took a bite of an apple: *our whole nature was corrupted. It darkened our understanding, weakened our will, and left in us a strong inclination to evil.* I was also severely warned against reading the stars in a Sunday newspaper, having my fortune told at the races, or believing that if a hen came into the kitchen with a straw on her tail it was a sign that a visitor could be expected. *It is also forbidden to give credit to dreams, fortune telling, incantations, charms, spells. All superstitions, observance of omens and accidents are also very sinful.* Under pain of grievous sin I was commanded *to pray for kings and all in high station*. And lest that were not enough it taught that *It is sinful to resist or combine against the established authorities or to speak with contempt or disrespect of those who rule over us.* To come to more personal matters I was warned *against all immodest songs, discourses, novels, comedies and plays and against all immodest looks, words or actions and everything that is contrary to chastity*. To bring home to my sinful nature how I should shun such occasions of sin I was informed a few pages on to beware of *lascivious looks or touches, idleness, bad company, all excesses in eating and drinking and whatever intends to inflame the passions*. To tell a jocose lie was also sinful. *No lie, jocose or otherwise can be lawful or innocent and no motive can excuse a lie, because a lie is always bad and sinful in itself.* This one I should pass on to Des MacHale, author of *The Book of Kerryman Jokes!* The penalties which our God handed out were severe. There was a General Judgment where I would be put on trial and if I committed any of the foregoing indiscretions and did not repent He would say to me: *Depart from me you cursed into everlasting fire which was prepared for the devil and his angels*, and then I would spend the rest of eternity in excruciating torment.

Now this is the kind of God I grew up with. Later in life when I studied philosophy I saw the absurdity of it, but despite all logical reasoning, I found it hard to shake off the deep impressions made upon me during those formative years. In a back corner of my mind I still saw my body as a vile thing, and God as a monster who was there to punish me, and it took many decades to rid myself of the notion of a theological God, created by man, and substitute a loving God created by Himself. The change happened this way:

A young Spanish priest named Juan Arias wrote an article for a Madrid daily newspaper, called *The God I Don't Believe In* and within weeks of its appearance he received thousands of letters from people in all walks of life, atheists, agnostics, drug addicts, alcoholics, prisoners, priests, contemplative nuns, all telling him how much the God he portrayed in the article had meant to them and how, like so many of us, they had been worshipping a false God all their lives. The article was expanded into a book and became a world best-seller in several languages. It was beautifully translated into English by Father Paul Barrett, O.F.M. Cap. of Cork and published as a paperback under the title of *The God I Don't Believe In*. When I read this book my whole relationship with God changed and at last I seemed to be able to throw off the heretical shackles imposed upon me by *Ecclesia Hiberniae*. Here is a very short extract which I never tire of reading:

I SHALL NEVER BELIEVE IN:
the God who catches man in a sin of weakness
the God who loves pain
the God who flashes a red light against human joys
the God who makes Himself the monopoly of a church,
  a race or a caste
the God who can only give a verdict with a rule-book in
  his hands
the God incapable of smiling at many of man's awkward
  mistakes

the God who 'sends' people to hell
the God who always demands 100% at examinations
the God incapable of forgiving what many men condemn
the God who does not accept a seat at our human festivities
the God who only the mature, the wise or the well-off can understand
the God who is adored by those who go to Mass yet go on stealing and calumniating
the aseptic God thought up by so many theologians and canonists in their ivory towers
the God for whom it is as sinful to enjoy the sight of a pair of pretty legs as to calumniate and rob one's neighbour and abuse one's power to get rich or take revenge
the God who says: 'You will pay for that'
the God who prefers injustices to disorder
the God who is happy with the man who gets down on his knees although he won't work
the God who is interested in souls and not in men
the God whose disciples turn their backs on the world's work and are indifferent to their brothers' story
the God who is preached by those priests who believe that hell is crowded and heaven almost empty
the God of those priests who say that everything and everybody can be criticised except themselves
the God who puts law before conscience
the God who prefers the rich and powerful
the God who accepts and endorses everything we priests say about him
the God who prefers purity to love
the God who cannot find Himself in the eyes of a child or a pretty woman or a mother in tears
the God who embraces politics
the God who destroys our flesh eternally instead of resurrecting it
the God for whom man is of value not for what he is but for what he has or for what he represents
the God who does not have the generosity of the sun which warms everything it touches, flowers as well as the manure heaps

the God in whom I cannot hope against all hope
YES, MY GOD IS THE OTHER GOD

I recall vividly the tremendous sense of excitement I felt when I read this young priest's book and contemplated his uplifting thoughts. A whole new world of positive beauty and joy opened out before me and God became an intelligent and loving reality. I slowly came to realise that a man's conscience is supreme, that he has to think for himself, and that Truth already dwells in his heart and not necessarily in some documents written thousands of years ago, edited, sub-edited and mutilated over the centuries, and interpreted by fallible human beings. The voice of God is within us, but for the most part we do not listen, since it is easier to pass the buck on to someone else and let him tell us what God is and what He wants us to do, and much more difficult to think clearly and read the words implanted in our own hearts. It has become a trifle trendy nowadays to declare oneself an atheist—it is the 'in' thing, along with beards, sidelocks, Edwardian dress, yo-yos and bubble-gum, yet in all the years of my life I have never met a real atheist. I have indeed met many who professed to be atheists because the only God they knew was a cruel God, a cynical God or an exploiter of human suffering, or an unconscious father figure, or a God of escapism, but I never met a human being who could honestly admit that there was no Totality outside of himself, that he was the be-all and end-all of life, for that is what atheism really means. I remember a science professor telling me that he could only believe in something if it could be seen and examined under his microscope, and that everything else had no existence. I knew this man well and knew that he had a very deep love for a charming wife and an invalid daughter. When I asked him if he really loved them he replied emphatically that he did, in a tone of voice that expressed indignation at the very idea of such a question.

'Can you put that love under your microscope and examine it?' I asked. There was a long silence and looking away into the distance he slowly and quietly replied: 'I guess I'm not a real atheist after all.' He was an honest man.

As we drew closer to the jagged Skellig Rocks it became clear that a landing would not be possible. Although the wind was moderate the swell and scend at the little pier was too strong, and if we were to tie up, *Dualla* could get a serious battering, with even the risk of being broken up. Indeed as we approached the opening we could see a figure, presumably one of the lighthouse men, running down the path waving his hands at us in gestures suggesting that we keep well away from the landing place. This was quite a disappointment. Our keenness to explore had been sharpened by Des Lavelle's first-class book *Skellig-Island Outpost of Europe*, but unfortunately, it would be both risky and dangerous, so we had to content ourselves with sailing around these precipitous rocks and admiring them from a safe offing. Some experts in the past have made a great mystery of the monastic settlement on the large Skellig, but I think a lot of this scholarly opinion can be taken with a grain of salt. Many amateurs now cast serious doubt on the theories of scholars and point out that the invention of carbon fourteen as a method of dating objects, proved that the opinions of these learned gentlemen in the past were completely misleading and well off the mark. Koestler may have been a little severe when he referred to 'the inertia of the professionals with a vested interest in tradition and in the monopoly of learning', yet I think it is advisable not to take scholarly conclusions too seriously and use one's own common sense. I find it hard to accept that there was ever a real full-time monastery on the Skelligs. It would have been possible for the monks to provide enough to eat. They could have fish, eggs, goats, sheep, fowl, and vegetables of many kinds could be grown in the arable patches, but one thing they simply could not provide enough of, and that was fuel. There is no fuel of any kind on the rock itself. From September to April, when the winter seas lash in all their fury, there are only about four or five days in that entire period when a landing would be possible, and taking into account this weather factor, the frail hide boats they used, I cannot see how anything like enough fuel could ever be landed to cook for a community, and to keep the many cells where monks could study, pray and sleep, in any kind of reasonable comfort. I believe the Skelligs was simply a summer retreat house and was vacated in the winter. But be that as it may, I think the only thing that is certain is that we will never really know. And that's as it should be; the men of the past are entitled to their secrets.

As *Dualla* rounded these two picturesque rocks, that looked like cathedrals of the sea designed by a heavenly architect, their sheer majesty overwhelmed me. In the presence of such lofty dignity and beauty the heart is sometimes moved to feelings of awe and fear mingled with veneration, and today these feelings were magnified by the thousands of gannets that circled around us, screaming in anger at our invasion of their privacy, and showering their unwanted visiting cards all over *Dualla's* deck. It must have been some such sight as this that inspired Hitchcock to give the world his masterly, but horrific film, *Birds*. But as we sailed away they saw that we meant no harm and, one by one, they dropped back to their loved ones on the ledges of the Little Skellig. Although the wind was only about force three *Dualla* got quite a buffeting from the backwash of the long Atlantic swell, and I was glad that it was not a point or two stronger, for if it were, it could be mighty unpleasant and indeed dangerous. More than one great ship was dashed to pieces here, and the old people will tell you that these crags are inhabited by a supernatural spirit, who, like the weeping maid of Lorelei, lures ships and sailors to their doom. One of the great near misses took place in the year 1779 when John Paul Jones, the famous American-French privateer, was becalmed off the Skelligs. This same gentleman was not too well loved in Kerry, for time and again his press-gang forced unwilling able-bodied men in Valentia and Dingle to crew his fleet. On this particular day his ship was the forty-two-gun *Bonhomme Richard*, so named as a compliment to his friend Benjamin Franklin who wrote *Poor Richard*. She was drifting perilously close to the Big Skelligs and was in grave danger of being dashed to pieces. Jones lowered his largest rowing boat, and twenty strong oarsmen rowed for more than two hours and towed the *Bonhomme Richard* until she was clear of the Rocks and out of danger. Then instead of returning to their ship the oarsmen cut the rope and rowed hell-for-leather for Ballinskelligs. You see, they were Kerrymen who some years before had been pressed into service by Jones, and now they broke free and were making for home. There was nothing Jones could do about it, except acknowledge defeat, and store in the back of his memory the knowledge that the man is not born yet who can outwit a bunch of Kerrymen.

Every monastic settlement, where men really shut themselves off from the world, becomes in time a place of pilgrimage visited by thousands, rarely to give anything, but always in the hope of getting something. This is not only true of Christians but also of every religion on the face of the earth and indeed it would be hard to blame the monks if they didn't turn an honest penny by catering for the spiritual and material needs of the greedy multitudes. The most enterprising I have ever come across was at a large monastery on the continent where the following price list appeared on the notice-board: *Mass by the Lord Abbot £5. Mass by the Assistant Abbot £4. Mass by the Prior £3. Mass by the Novice Master £2. Mass by a Community Father £1.* These holy men catered for the needs of everyone, high or low, rich or poor.

Although rather inaccessible the Skellig Rock became a notable place of pilgrimage and one can still see the remains of the Penitential Path and the ruins of the old Stations of the Cross. In the fifteenth century a writer named Thaddeus Moynihan told us: *This rocke standes three leagues from the earthe in the main ocean. It is seven hundred perches long or high, and with much adoe one man at a tyme may climb the stayres to it. If he lookes at any syde he will be afrayd of falling into the sea. At the toppe of this rocke is a church built, and a churchyarde about it, people coming from afar to performe a pilgrimage in that Rocke.*

But for some rather strange reason pilgrimages to the Skelligs became associated with love and marriage, and in the later years the pilgrims were mainly young men and women eligible for wedlock. They were supposed to perform the various penitential exercises, but human nature being what it is, they were found more often amid the crevices and crags enjoying themselves in other ways. Finally these pilgrimages were denounced from every altar by bell, book, and candle, but it was only the intervention of the police that finally put a stop to them. But things like that are hard to suppress — they keep bouncing back in a variety of other forms — and in this case they emerged in a form known as Skelligs Lists. These were defamatory songs, some also very scurrilous, in which unmarried men and maidens were lampooned and advised to make a pilgrimage to the Skelligs. Delicacy was not a high point as this one shows:

> *The Hegarty lad*
> *From Strand Street bohaun*
> *Is there with his Mary tonight*
> *The Abbot of Skellig*
> *Will wed them at dawn —*
> *A wedding that cannot be white.*

And another more prosaic:

The shades of old spectres emerged from the mountain
The moonbeams were dancing on lone Sammy's Rock
When a shriek of dismay brought our eyes on Kate Foley
For the tar from a boat had spoilt Katy's best frock.
Poor Kate was all out for her one night of glory
And had planned now for months to besiege Tracy's heart
But now her best weapon was damaged and useless
The bow that she brought to shoot broke Cupid's dart.

These 'lists' were printed in the Cork and Kerry areas and there is a letter from an irrate parent to a Cork publisher dated 28 January 1834:

Sir,
 You are requested to take notice that I will hold you responsible for any liberties taken with the names of

Mary Ellen Harris, Sarah Harris and Eliza Driscoll, they being members of my family, and having received intelligence of some person or persons wishing to expose them in Skelligs Lists which are to come to and through your press, I am determined to indict all persons concerned if there is anything prejudicial to their person, interest or character in any manner.

Yours truly,
Hugh Driscoll

When we left the Skelligs behind us we set our course for Bray Head at the south west tip of Valentia Island, leaving the lonely Lemon Rock inside us and a nasty tidal race where the sea bed suddenly shoals, well outside us. The steely, rocky shores, from which the quartz sparkled like diamonds, were surrounded by high naked cliffs and sunburned hills. The wind was rising, tattered clouds began to dash across the sunlit sky, and the foam on the crests of the waves gleamed a brilliant white, as we tore along through the surging seas. Passing the wild picturesque St Finians Bay I thought of what a strange man the same Finian was and how his harsh outlook dominated the early Irish Church. He was the author of a famous *Penitential* which was inhuman, sadistic, totally unchristian and obsessed with matters of sex. A man or woman who commits adultery must fast on bread and water only for one year and during that period was forbidden to make love to his or her spouse. The same penance applied to anyone who gave an aphrodisiac to another to arouse sexual passions. An unfortunate nun who gives birth to a child must fast on bread and water for six years, but the responsible gentleman gets away with three years. Married couples are forbidden to have intercourse on Saturday and Sunday nights and for three periods of forty days each year. These are but a few of his brutal rules. There's a local tradition which says that St Finian was so cross-eyed that no woman would look at him and that, as a last resort, he became a monk. This may explain his neurotic preoccupation with sexual offences. However, a bit of his stupid thinking dominated the Irish church for centuries, and so alienated the Irish males away from females, that an Irish queer came to be defined as a man who preferred women to drink. It is alright for us in this day and age to laugh at such nonsense but in its time it was taken seriously, and must have caused untold human suffering. The early Irish church tended to make the faithful live by rules and not by love. This in its way is quite understandable since educational facilities were virtually nonexistant, except around monastic settlements. Indeed for the first three or four centuries after the coming of Patrick the church was centered in, and organised, around these monasteries. Our concept of a monastery is a place of holiness and contemplation, where men devote themselves to a life of self-denial and intimate union with God. It was not so in those early centuries. Monasteries were centres of power, owning vast acres of land which were rented out to hundreds of tenants. The greater portion of the monks were married and lived with their wives and families in close proximity to the main buildings. They attended divine office and prayers, but for the most part, they were engaged in work supporting the community. They were teachers, craftsmen, builders, carpenters, farmers, scribes, and indeed good fighters, for they might have to go to battle with other monasteries over some land dispute—more than one inter-monastery battle is recorded where hundreds of monks were killed. There was an important restriction imposed on these married monks which limited them to have only one wife each. Polygamy was the accepted norm at the time but, as a gesture of self-denial, the monks were obliged to stay with one woman. In most cases less than ten percent of the inhabitants of a monastery were ordained priests or ascetics, who lived a life of prayer, meditation and holiness. Indeed in many cases the abbot himself was a married man and was able to pass on the abbacy to one of his sons. In other cases strong personalities came to the top like St Columban, St Ciaran, St Finian, St Brendan and in the case of convents St Ita, St Brigid, and their writings and thinking dominated their weaker brethren. It was in this way that the savage Rule of St Columban and also St Finian came to be accepted, but in fairness, it should be said that various popes condemned these rules and finally replaced them altogether with something more Christian and humane.

As we sailed along this beautiful coastline I recalled the great monasteries that dotted the whole Iveragh Peninsula: Derrynane, Ballinskelligs, Temple Cashel, Killabuonia, Kildrenagh, Kildreelig, and many more, and the islands like the Skelligs and Church Island, where the ascetics retreated in summer away from the hurly-burly of normal monastic activities, to make their souls.

As *Dualla* sailed past Puffin Island there was a wild scattering on all sides of those quaint comical little birds. There is something strangely droll about the puffin, something which provokes laughter, yet you do not seem to be laughing at them but with them. Their blue, yellow and red beaks, bright orange feet, merry twinkly eyes and awkward half-wings make them look like comedians in a circus. They spend the long winter months out in the Atlantic, hidden away from the curious eye of man, and return here to Kerry to breed and hatch their young. Each puffin lays one egg only, which is hatched by both father and mother in turn and after thirty-five days the young puffin appears. Then as winter approaches, when it is strong and healthy, it disappears with thousands of others back out into the Atlantic, until the soft winds of spring call them home again. As Bray Head came abeam we ran into a nasty race caused by the rising wind blowing against the ebbing tide, and this unpleasant water lasted all the way until Valentia harbour opened up. We started the engine, lowered the sails, motored in past the lighthouse on Cromwell Point, and dropped anchor in two fathoms of calm water just south east of Knightstown pier. It was six o'clock in the evening.

I think every yachtsman experiences a feeling of relief when he is safely anchored in a new harbour. You could not describe the feeling as a sense of achievement, but rather a sense of relaxation, a sense of rest. No matter how much a man loves the sea he yearns to be back on the land, to reach the safety and security of a harbour, to come home again. Having tidied up the sails, launched the punt, and scrubbed *Dualla's* deck to remove the gannett's emblems, we opened a bottle of wine and sat out in the cockpit while the dinner was cooking, enjoying the peace and tranquility of the sunlit harbour, chatting and making small talk about anything that crossed our minds. After about half an hour or so I heard several sharp blasts of a motor horn and, when I looked around, I saw two females waving to us from the pier. They were our two young German friends from Derrynane and of course they had their car. It was all pre-arranged, and with genuine sincerity I complimented my two companions on their excellent organisation and foresight. The girls joined us for dinner and afterwards drove us across the new bridge into Portmagee, and then several miles on to the mainland, to a singing pub of particular charm which they had discovered.

We arrived a little early and the singing had not yet begun. The spacious lounge was more than half-full, and I could see that it was not a pub that catered especially for tourists. I judged that the majority of those present were locals, the men in their three piece suits, their hair glistening with brillantine, their faces shining and smelling of carbolic soap. My two companions and the young Germans went over to a corner where there was some kind of a game to be played, and I found a place for myself beside a dapper little man in his mid-fifties, with a thin ascetic face, rimless glasses and a growth of down on his baldy head like a freshly plucked chicken ready for the oven. After a few false starts we struck up a conversation together, but he was rather shy and diffident and gave me the impression of a man who, for the most part of his life, had gone the same way to work, met the same people, said the same things and watched the same friends growing slowly old. How wrong I was and how right was one William Shakespeare that 'there's no art to find the minds construction in the face.' When we had taken a few more drinks and exhausted the weather and the state of the world as topics, he explained that he was a medical specialist from a large English city spending a holiday here in Kerry. He was originally from the west of Ireland and had spent more than twenty-five years in England, but he never failed to come back every year for his holidays. He told me his christian name was Theophilus, a strange name for an Irishman, he said, but his mother was a great reader of *Old Moore's Almanac* and she called him after Old Moore himself. I was trying to figure out what kind of specialist he was. Eye? Ear? Throat? or what? Eventually after another few drinks it all came out, and he was off at full steam. He had a lucrative contract, he said, from all the hospitals in a large English city to shave men's behinds before an operation. 'Any blockage, stoppage, piles or other obstruction and I am on my way with razor and brush. My client kneels on the bed with his head on the pillow, and his behind up as high as it can go. It's not an easy job to shave them in that particular area, especially if they have piles, since it's hard to get the razor around them little knolls and if you make one slip it can have very serious consequences But I'm doing it for twenty-five years now and I'm recognised by all the leading surgeons as a top specialist. Indeed I consider myself as important as they are for, if somebody doesn't open the half-door how can you let the cat out.'

'Do you not find it a little bit unpalatable to be looking all day long at that particular part of man's body?' I asked, trying to keep serious.

'Ah,' he answered, 'you get used to it and 'tis interesting enough, for no two different valleys is the same, and when you're getting a fiver a shave, you don't worry to much about the scenery. Of course there are odd times when it isn't all that nice, especially when you have to attend to a farmer who hasn't washed himself since his mother changed his nappy, or maybe a butcher given to breaking wind. But on the other hand you do see some strange objects and the thought often crosses your mind that there are more than seven wonders in the world. I can assure you I have seen some funny shapes and sizes dangling in my time, and it isn't all ordinary people I do. I've shaved bishops, dukes, royalty, TV personalities, soccer stars, film actors – you name it I've shaved it – and I can tell you they have no special privileges in that part of their body. If the women who are inclined to swoon when they see TV stars saw what I see they wouldn't have any cause for swooning! 'Tisn't the same way the sun shines in the parlour as in the kitchen, and there are very few sights I see that would be a cause of confession for man or woman. But do you know, when I get real depressed with life I go along to a confirmation and see the bishop dressed up in all his regalia, or maybe to a duke opening a garden fete, and I think of the little job I did on them, and then all the depression vanishes.'

'If you were starting life again,' I asked without even a smile, 'would you take up the same profession?'

'Of course I would,' he answered. 'I'm an expert at my work and when you become an expert at anything there's great job satisfaction in it. Do you know that I once wrote to the British Management Institute and offered to give a talk at one of their seminars on Job Satisfaction? They declined my offer on the grounds that the majority of members were executives and my particular skills would not have a direct lesson for them. I believe that God in his wisdom created certain men for certain jobs, and I know that this is the only job I'd ever be happy at. By the way if ever you come over to England look me up and I'll bring you along on a day's work with me. I'll give you a white coat and you can hold the shaving mug and towel and I'll tell them you're my new assistant.' In that moment I knew that whatever dates I might fail to keep, this was one I would certainly turn up for.

By now the singing had started. Two young men were playing a gadget and a guitar, helped out by a lady vocalist. Soon the crowd began to sing too, and here and there the young girl cajoled members of the audience into singing a song of their own. In this way I heard quite a number of songs that I had never heard before. One country girl gave a delightful account of a married woman of the past telling her husband what she had to do:

At six o'clock each morning when to work you do go
I have to rise and light the fire and the bellows for to blow
I have to set the breakfast things and get the kettle boiled.
Besides, you know, I have to wash and dress the youngest child.

When breakfast it is over, you know, I made a rule
To get the children ready and send them off to school.
I have to shake and make the beds and sweep the room also
And then clean the windows and empty the chamber po.

I have to wash the sheets and blankets, the pinafores and frocks
Gowns, petticoats and pillow slips, skirts handkerchiefs and socks
I have to nurse the infant and wash the napkins too.
There's no man can imagine what a woman has to do.

Four times a day I have to cook your wants to supply
Breakfast, dinner, tea and supper, I have to stew and fry.
I hardly get a moment's rest I have to run here and there.
Then I have to scrub the tables down likewise the stools and chairs.

Some men will curse their wives, and kick them, it is true
But a man without a woman whatever would he do
So, men if you would happy be don't treat your wives with shame
For when a woman does her best she cannot be to blame.

Not to be outdone a fine strapping Kerryman stood up and gave his answer to the previous song:

I'm a poor unlucky married man, I've such an awful wife
I please her, I do all I can, but still she plagues my life.
I try to please her day and night but she treats me like a sow
Each morning I must the fire light or there's bound to be a row.

She wakes me in the morning an awful cruel way
She kicks me out upon the floor, not a cross word dare I say.
I must wash the sheets and blankets and my socks and shirt I vow
And if I don't wash hers as well there's bound to be a row.

She's taken in a lodger and he's single bye the bye
She says I must make room and on the other side of him lie.
They eat meat, give me the bones—that don't look right
somehow
But if I dare to grumble, there's bound to be a row.

He takes her out to balls and plays, and often stay till morn
While I must sit and nurse the kids, and wait for their return
When she rings the bell I let her in and to her make a bow
But if I ask her where she was there's bound to be a row.

She often gives a party to her cousins seven or eight
And I must hurry home from work, the table for to wait.
I carry dishes in till the sweat runs down my brow
And if I chance to break a plate, there's bound to be a row.

And when I've earned my wages, after working all the week
I turn in every penny up and then she has the cheek
To give me twopence to myself, for that I have to bow
And if I spend it all at once, there's bound to be a row.

The pub was now crowded, the noise made conversation impossible as song after song and chorus after chorus was sung, and then just before closing time the young girl who was conducting the music and singing came over to my friend of the razor, Theophilus, and called on him to give the last song. Evidently this was a pattern and he had done so many times before. He stood up on a stool and in a genteel voice gave a Kerry version of an old classic:

There was a young Tralee man who went to meet his dear
The moon was shining brightly and the stars were viewing
clear
He went to his love's window and he called her by her name
Then she rose and let him in and went back to bed again.

Saying: 'Patsy, dearest Patsy, tonight will be your doom
Strip off onto your naked pelt there's no one in the room
The streets they are too lonely for you to walk about
So, come, squeeze me in your arms, love, and blow the
candle out.

My father and my mother next bedroom they do lie
Kissing and canoodling and why not you and I?
Kissing and canoodling without a fear or doubt

So, come toss me in your arms, love, and blow the candle out.

It was nine months and after, nine months ago today
He wrote to me a letter saying he was far away:
He wrote to me a letter that fickle Kerry lout
And he never said when he'd come back to blow the candle out.

Come all you gallant Irish girls pay heed to what I say
Never court a Kerryman who sails the far off sea
For some day or another with a grin upon his mouth
He'll do to you what he did to me when he blew the candle out.

In the dimly-lit street after closing time the singing continued incoherently and drunkenly as the singers straggled homewards. I said goodbye to Theophilus, congratulated him on his song and on the excellent work I was sure he was doing in his professional field. As I was moving towards the car, where the boys and girls were waiting for me, he tapped me on the shoulder and said: 'By the way in fairness I should tell you that Theophilus is not my name. You see, you can never trust a stranger, for the man that's crooked in this village is sure to be crooked in the next. I couldn't take chances, for maybe you're one of them tax-collectors or worse still, maybe you're one of them fellows that does be writing books. Anyway, good night, and may your goat never back away from the puck,' and he disappeared into the darkness.

The next morning we awoke to find the sun spilling its comforting heat on the calm waters of the harbour. There was not even a breath of wind and the sea looked like a glazed pavement. The tiny wavelets rolled in bubbling ripples upon the pebbles of the beach making an elfin fringe of foam upon the water. In the distance the horizon was hidden in a veil of misty blue. We would stay in Valentia until the following day. The boys managed to borrow a punt and had planned with the two girls to go exploring around Begenish, Church Island and the Caher River. I, for my part, wanted to go meandering around Valentia with Maxie.

After a late breakfast I brought him ashore in the rubber punt, and we strolled along the ege of the sea towards the little Catholic church. The first time I ever visited Valentia was during World War II, and I was then told a great story about this little church. It appears that many many years before, the Redemptorists were preaching a mission there, and as was their usual practice, were pouring fire and brimstone on all and sundry. After the best part of a week of this, the unfortunate islanders had been worked into a state of near frenzy. On the last evening the preacher was painting a most lurid picture of the sufferings of hell. He kept emphasising that in hell there would be perpetual weeping and gnashing of teeth, with the emphasis on this gnashing of teeth. One poor old woman, completely overcome by emotion, drew back the shawl off her head and spoke up to the missioner. 'What will I do, Father? I have no teeth?' A titter of laughter ran through the church. 'Silence in the House of God!' bellowed the preacher. 'And as for you, my good woman,' he said pointing at her, 'you need have no worries. In hell teeth will be provided!'

This church, a few minutes walk down the road from the pier, is a delightful old-world building that invites you to pray. Inside I felt a deep sense of peace as I knelt down near the door and rested my head in my hands. There wasn't a sound except the patter of Maxie's feet as he wandered around slightly bewildered in such strange surroundings. I was alone except for a young lady who knelt in one of the front seats in a reverential attitude of prayer. After a few minutes I made my way back outside, just in time, I think, to prevent Maxie from misbehaving himself in the hallowed precincts. While I was admiring the belfry, which looked as if it were an imitation of an ancient Irish round tower, the young lady who was praying appeared. I was at once startled by her beauty—tall, elegant, well-built, reddish hair, in her mid- or late thirties, dressed simply in slacks and sweater.

'What a beautiful dog,' she exclaimed as she saw Maxie.

'I was admiring him in the church.'

'Thank you,' I replied somewhat stuck for words. I felt a strange sensation in her presence, a pleasant shock which only the eyes of a unique woman can give, a sudden physical attraction as if some unknown force impelled me towards her, and made me feel as if I had known her all my life. All this happened in a few seconds. I was tongue-tied but very gently she started a conversation about the church, the strand, the island, the people. She was not only beautiful but intelligent as well, and as we strolled back towards the pier I lost my shyness and found my tongue under the beguiling spell of her tender eyes, her merry dimples, and the soft graciousness of her voice. When we reached the pier I invited her on board *Dualla* for a drink and, without showing the slightest hesitation, she accepted. We rowed out in the punt, and when we were safely on board, I opened a bottle of wine, and we began to exchange confidences and to converse freely on those personal topics which are always a preliminary to a better understanding between two people. Sheila was her name and she lived in Dublin, she told me, and worked there in what I understood to be some form of public relations. South Kerry was her favourite part of Ireland and, for the third time, she was holidaying here with Waterville as her base. Valentia, she thought, was one of the more delightful localities, and she had only recently discovered the magnificent walks along the cliffs and the breathtaking views from Valentia Heights. I told her about myself who I was, where I came from and what I did. Yes, she then remembered that she had read my book *Tomorrow To be Brave* some years ago and her joy at meeting me was quite unconcealed. This I found both strange and unusual, because most women who read that book and who subsequently meet me look upon me with a mixture of fright and awe as if I were a strange being from another planet. When I told her this she laughed impishly and said that if a man shared his life with a woman the most natural thing in the world was to write a book about her.

They say that when two lonely people meet and start

talking that neither becomes aware of how fast time flies, and indeed this was quite true of us. It was only when we began to feel the slightest twinge of hunger that we realised early afternoon was upon us, so I opened another bottle of wine, set a table of brown bread, cold meats and salads, and together we dined, oddly enough, in silence. It was as if we had already spoken too much.

She had a car on the pier and she suggested that we take a little trip around the island for the afternoon. I accepted with enthusiasm and with a great joy filling my heart. In the short time I was with her the whole world seemed to have changed and my soul became enveloped in a delightful sense of peace and harmony. Was this love at first sight? Or was it but a passing infatuation? I do not know. Some of the deepest moments of life are locked doors to which we only find the key when it is too late.

We brought Maxie with us and he coiled up quietly on the back seat of the car, totally indifferent to the beauties of Valentia or to the romantic mood of his master. We drove first to look at the old cable station and Sheila recalled a connection between the island and a very famous Betty Davis film *All This And Heaven Too*. This film was the story of Henriette Desportes, who entered the service of Duc de Praslin in Paris as governess, and who seven years later was tried for complicity with the Duc in the murder of his wife. She was acquitted and later married Henry Field, a minister of religion who stood by her through all her troubles. It was Henry Field's brother, Cyrus, who was the principle engineer in the laying of the transatlantic cable from USA to Valentia. We drove along through the little village of Chapeltown and then towards Port Magee, but instead of turning over the bridge we continued straight on and after a short distance parked the car and went for a walk towards the magnificent cliffs of Bray Head. Strolling together side by side along the edge of the Atlantic, amid the wild beauty of the island throbbing with life, seemed but to heighten the feeling that we each knew that we understood the other and there was a bond of mysterious dimension being moulded between us. Set against the background of the sea her physical beauty was striking. Every curve of her body was a temptation. The sun shimmering in her hair, gave her an other-world bewitching appearance. All I longed to do was to walk along with her arm in arm listening to the beating of my heart and mingling my feelings with the sensuous beauty of the day. Like myself, she loved nature, the changing skies, the flight of the gulls, the play of the sunlight on cliffs and sea. On and off, after intervals of silences, we chatted about life, literature, art, music, the sea, supermarkets, pop-songs and any wise or foolish thing that came into our heads.

After a detour we returned to the car and now drove back the little winding road towards Valentia Heights. The road up to this majestic spot looks quite dangerous, but only in so far as it is almost too narrow for cars to pass each other and on one side, there is a sheer drop of hundreds of feet to the sea, but today there was no danger as we were the only car around. Up at the top there are the sad, mournful remains of the once famous Valentia Quarries, now turned into an impressive grotto. We sat down near the edge of the road enjoying a view which must be almost unrivalled in the whole of Ireland. Far away out to sea the towering Blasket Islands surrounded by a host of jagged dangerous rocks, in the distance the Kerry mountains with their patches of yellow whin and blue heather gleaming in the sun, while the little paths, like coloured ribbons, ran down the rugged slopes. Far below us lay the wide mottled surface of the sea which seemed to sleep beneath the warm sun, the moist lips of the little waves hardly breaking on the shore, and over all a clear, blue untroubled sky. We sat there just chatting and musing and from time to time enjoying one of those sympathetic silences between people who no longer have to talk to each other to be happy. Later we came back along the cliff road and turned down a narrow byway to the harbour and the woods of Glanleam.

Glanleam is the only wooded part of the island mainly because it was once the home of the Knights of Kerry, that breed of English landlords to whom wealth was no object, abundance a way of life, and who ruled the destinies of the unfortunate Irish with a fist of iron. Sheila recalled a story an old islander once told her about an eviction in the bad days towards the end of the last century. A poor widow with five children was evicted from her home and when the bailiff came she had a cake baking on the fire. She asked the bailiff to wait until the cake was baked so that she could feed her starving children. He refused and kicked the cake and the fire out into the yard and seized the house. Late that night the unfortunate widow stole back to see if she could get a few potatoes from her garden to feed the children, who were by now weak with the hunger in the side of the ditch. The bailiff caught her, tied her to a tree and left her there all night.

We parked the car and strolled through the beautiful private woods, without asking for permission. Whenever I invade the grounds of one of 'our betters' and am challenged, I have a fool-proof technique. I pretend I know no English and I speak Irish only. This invariably works, since these people can usually speak no second language. After a few unsuccessful attempts to communicate, it becomes so exasperating that I am allowed to wander at will. But today we met no one as we strolled along through the archways of overhanging branches and listened to the blackbirds in the laurels fluting their earth-sweet songs. The ivy clung to the tortured twisted barks of the old trees, flowers peeped out from the bushes, the violets tinted the edges of the paths, looking up with their shy blue eyes, while the perfume relaxed the air around us. The earth was heavy with age as we lightly trod the fallen leaves of time. We were searching for a fuchsia bush, which Sheila had heard was the largest in Europe, with a circumference of one hundred and fifty yards. But we did not find it so we left Glanleam behind us as the evening sun was touching the lovely trees with its golden light. The afternoon had passed so quickly it was hard to realise that it was now well past seven o'clock Impulsively I invited Sheila to dinner in a Waterville hotel, and she accepted with unaffected naturalness.

We ate our meal and drank our wine in silence, perhaps tired from the long intimate and trusting talks we had had all day. The little orchestra was playing Strauss music ever so softly. The candlelight cast a strange magical spell all round the room. The whole atmosphere touched deeply on the emotions, bringing to the surface those strange sensations that defy explanation. When you feel in this kind of mood you begin to understand why the stars are in the sky, why the sun shines, why the birds sing, why love is beauty, and beauty is love. There was an unfamiliar beat in my heart, a sensation of fright creeping over me, and an overpowering urge to speak and tell her everything that was in my soul.

As we were having our last glass of wine I decided to open up, even though in that moment I felt myself incredibly stupid.

'Sheila,' I said, 'there is something I have to say to you.'

'I know,' she answered with a wonderful smile as she gently rested her hand on mine. 'You are going to tell me that you think you have fallen in love with me and that you want to spend the rest of your days at my side. That is the nicest thing any man could say to me but, please, don't say it—I could very easily say, yes—and if I did I would only be letting my imagination destroy what is, for a dream of what might only be. Sometimes the love that's not expressed is the love that lasts longest. The endearment of this afternoon can soothe the heart without enslaving it, can live on as a beautiful memory. So listen carefully, because I have not told you all my story. I was once married in North America. I had a young son three years old. Through sheer boredom I had an affair with another man and when my husband found out he packed his bags and rushed from the house, taking my little son with him, and drove up country to where his mother lived. He must have been wildly agitated, for less than half way there, he crashed the car at a level-crossing and both of them were killed. From that moment on I knew I was a murderer. I came back home to

Ireland and tried to pick up the threads of my life and begin anew, but I was forever haunted to the depths of my soul by the terrible happenings of the past. Slowly time began to heal and, about a year ago, when I thought some sanity had come into my life, I found out I had leukaemia and my days were numbered. It is now July. I will be dead before Christmas.'

She spoke with an absolute calm and assurance as if it were the most natural thing in the world.

'Please let things be,' she pleaded, 'let today be a beautiful rose in a world of a thousand thorns. The shadow of things is always more exquisite than the substance. Any other way I might not be able to face what's coming, and you would only find acute and prolonged suffering for a second time in your life.' Then after a short pause she continued: 'We will talk no more about it. It's time to go. Let me drive you back to *Dualla*. Please try to understand.'

We drove along the narrow road in silence, the headlights of the car playing strange tricks with the barren wasted countryside. She put a cassette into her player and said: 'Let's listen to a symphony by Brahms. I prefer him to Beethoven. Brahms speaks to the heart. Beethoven speaks to the soul.' The ethereal music helped to calm my confused and bewildered mind and we drove along in silence until we reached Knightstown Pier. In the darkness we walked side by side, hand in hand, down to the steps where the punt was tied. When we stopped I gazed up at the millions of stars twinkling like will-o'-the-wisps in the night sky and mirrored in the still calm water.

'Are your thoughts in this moment worth a penny?' she asked with a smile. 'I was thinking of a verse of poetry by Francis Thompson,' I answered. 'I do not know why it should come to my mind just now.'

'Say it for me,' she whispered.

Still looking at the stars I quoted:

> *The fairest things have fleetest end:*
> *Their scent survives their close;*
> *But the rose's scent is bitterness*
> *To him that loves the rose.*

She went her unremembering way,
She went, and left in me
The pang of all the partings gone
And partings yet to be.

She left me marvelling why my soul
Was sad that she was glad:
At all the sadness in the sweet,
The sweetness in the sad.

After a moment's silence she took my head in her hands and gave me the gentlest kiss on the lips. Then she was gone. I watched the lights of her car as they shone through the village, and then my eyes followed them up and down in the darkness until they disappeared altogether.

I rowed out to *Dualla*, Maxie sitting in the stern, his big wonderful eyes looking up at me. The boys had not yet returned. I slowly went to bed. I could not think. I could not sleep. Maxie gently jumped on to the bunk, and crept up quietly and rested his furry head on my shoulder as if to say 'I understand'.

Only once before in my life had I known a woman of supreme courage. Sheila was the second. Less than four months later she was dead. There was no funeral. She donated her body to medical research.

5

The next morning we awoke to find the harbour enveloped in a mist that rested like a shroud of death on the water. It was not a fog, but a summer haze, yet it blotted out the sun and the sky, and reduced visibility to a few hundred yards. I finished my breakfast sitting mournfully in the cockpit, depressed in spirit and heavy in heart. The old Irish poets always introduced an element into their poetry called

Chomhbhrón na Nadúra (The Sympathy of Nature). In their poems they made nature reflect the dejected, cheerless moods of the human spirit, and this morning it was happening all around me. Among the many confused thoughts going through my head was the terrible law of life that we have to lose something when we thought we had found it. How delightful it would be, I reflected, if the end of everything were as pleasant as the beginning. But no, the end is always sad. Emptiness replaces joy and hope. A thing of beauty vanishes and only the memory remains.

I had to pull myself together lest my mood become contagious and affect the two boys. There is one inflexible rule on *Dualla*: whoever is moody or liverish must leave the boat forthwith, so I put on my best Dale Carnegie smile and whistled the tune they were singing while washing up. After a short while we took council together and decided that, despite the haze, we would make for Dingle. As there was no wind we started the engine, hauled the anchor and slipped away out into the open sea.

We set a compass course for Eask Tower, which marks the entrance to Dingle Harbour, so when we cleared Dolus Head we put *Dualla* on compass and ourselves in the good hands of the Almighty, for in a matter of ten or fifteen minutes we had lost sight of all land and were alone as if we had quit the world, with only the mist and the fog surrounding us. I took the wheel and kept my eyes on the frail compass-needle which was pointing a little east of north. This should bring us dead on to our destination, only twelve miles away, and which we should easily reach in a matter of two hours. The boys stayed up on deck and kept a sharp look out for trawlers or other boats likely to cross our path, and which, in the bad visibility, could easily stike us down. There is a terrible sense of solitude about fog or mist at sea, and one feels lost to the rest of the world which cannot be sensed or seen, so in order to ease the aloneness we turned the radio on loud, and managed to hit a programme of silly pop songs which went a long way towards relieving our isolation and reminding us that there were others on the earth besides ourselves, and in this way we coasted steadily towards Dingle Harbour. But now a new problem had arisen affecting the rest of the cruise. As a result of a telephone message the evening before, the two boys learned that they would have to leave me at Dingle, and go to Dublin for some interviews in connection with their examinations. This was a major setback, for we had planned to call at all the harbours on the Kerry coast, visit the Magharee Islands and end our cruise at Tarbert near the mouth of the Shannon. Because of this new development I had to change my plans. I would now spend a night in Dingle, and if weather permitted, a night on the Great Blasket, and then return as quickly as I could to Derrynane, or if possible, to Castletownbere. The reason for all this is simple. It would be too dangerous for me to cruise alone north of the Blasket Sound, mainly because of the scarcety of safe harbours. The Sound itself is a most treacherous stretch of water, with extra strong tides, that could easily sweep a yacht on to the numerous submerged rocks which literally dot this whole area. Between Clogher Head and Dunmore Head there is also a perilous tidal race, both on the ebb and on the flood. More often than not, storms hit this coast before the meteorological office has time to forecast them. Again, the harbours north of the Sound are by no means safe. Smerwick Harbour is comfortable enough in a south-west wind but if it blew up from the north-west, which it often does during the night, then it could be impossible for a man on his own to get out of the narrow entrance. Even if he did get out where could he go? There is no real shelter from a north-west gale anywhere nearer than Fenit, twenty-five miles away, and at the best of times Fenit is a very awkward anchorage. The same applies to Brandon Harbour—it is completely exposed to the north. So is Scraggane Bay. Now I would not mind all this if I had the two boys with me, to change sails, to take the wheel, to put her about, or to effect a repair if something gave way. *Dualla* herself could stand any seas, but to handle her alone in a storm, so near such a forbidding coast would be too much for me. I could not do without help and so I decided to keep to waters where I could run quickly to a safe harbour from all winds, to get in without difficulty and stay there in the secure knowledge that I was protected from every side. By such decisions do yachtsmen stay alive.

We were only about an hour and a half out from Valentia, when the mist began to lift, letting the sun shine through, and we were able to pick out Eask Tower on the summit of Carhoo Hill. There was still no wind so we kept motoring, and shortly afterwards entered Dingle Harbour between Reenbeg and Beenbane points. Dingle is a magnificent and safe harbour, but its great drawback is that it is too shallow for a yacht to anchor. The only place where there is enough water at all stages of the tide is nearly a mile away from the town, so the best thing to do is to tie up at the pier where, near the end, there is enough depth. Somewhat west of Foheragh Point there is a dredged channel and the marks for this are: Flahive's pub in line with the outer edge of the pier. So we kept strictly to this course and arrived safely at the quay, where we tied up alongside a large trawler, covered with nets, fish boxes and other paraphernalia. We had barely made fast when a small fishing boat pulled in above us. They had a box of plaice and an exceptionally large skate. One of the fishermen cut open the skate and extracted a whole plaice from its insides. He then threw the plaice into the box with the rest of the fish. I made a mental note not to buy any plaice in Dingle that day.

The July sun was beaming down softly on this pleasant landlock harbour. Dingle itself seemed full of joyous, carefree life. Gay resplendent cars, with windows and sun-roofs open, moved up and down the road to Dunquin and Slea Head. Lightly clad tourists, with sun-hats and cameras, mingled through the fishermen sorting out their nets and lobster pots on the pier. The boys were sad and depressed at the idea of leaving. They admitted they had not often seen such a collection of beautiful and unattached young girls strolling around. The whole mood of the place contrasted so strangely with the eerie silence of mist and sea that had enveloped us for the past few hours. We had a quick lunch and, with heavy hearts, the boys prepared to leave. Just ahead of us there was a large plastic yacht, with every imaginable gadget and flag on full display. As we came in earlier we noticed quite a few on board, sitting around drinking and eating cocktail sausages like woodflies on fresh horse-manure. The owner condescended to nod to us as we passed, and now he strolled down the pier to have a closer look. He was like a toad in uniform, dressed in reefer jacket and club buttons, dark flannels and black patent shoes, open-necked white shirt with a red scarf casually peeping out, a cigar in his well-fed mouth. He was followed at some distance by what seemed to be his wife, a plump chatter-box, with the paunch of a prelate, and a look as if she had the brains of a grasshopper. She was accompanied by a rather gaunt virginal looking female of uncertain years, which reminded one of a portrait by Gainsborough that had faded through too much exposure to sunlight. He peered down rather disdainfully at us, at the unwashed dishes in a yellow basin, at a teapot upon the coach-roof, at a pot of potato skins on the transom, at a bra which the boys captured from one of the German girls, pinned onto the rigging like a trophy of war, at a half-cut barm-brack resting on a tin of diesel. After a few seconds he set his head aloft like a mongrel sniffing better things and moved away followed by the two dames still chatting.

When I had said farewell to the boys, I tidied up on deck, washed the utensils and made *Dualla* look a bit more respectable. I shaved, freshened myself up, and went ashore followed closely by Maxie. There was great life and activity all around. At the town end of the pier a pedlar with a dray-cart full of second-hand clothes was trying to sell his wares to a group of Kerry farmers crowded around him.

'Come on now, me fine decent men,' he was saying. 'I didn't come here to stick me hand into ye'r pockets but to do ye a favour, to sell ye the finest cloth this side of the Magillicuddy Reeks and to turn ye into gentlemen so that the neighbours would be nudging one another on the way to last Mass and saying that 'tis how ye were after getting a lob of money from America. Now look at this suit of clothes! Ye heard about it, ye read about it and here it is! 'Tis a suit as smooth as the skin of a cat, a suit that's so good that 'twould see any man to the grave. He'd never have to buy another.'

'How much are you looking for it, in one word?' asked a tall angular farmer, with a cap on the side of his head, and an adams apple which moved up and down like the piston of an engine.

'Remember, I'm not sellin' it,' replied the pedlar, 'I'm givin' it away as a handsel—twenty-five pounds—and you could get married in it.'

'Oh wisha that would be the marriage without the kisses. I suppose you think 'tis a lot of soft fools let out from the poor house you have around you. There isn't a man or woman born that would get as much from you as would break their fast without payin' three times over for it. Was it from King Philip of England you bought it that you're askin' so much for it?' Take five pounds and be glad to get it.'

'Oh Glory be to God and His Blessed Mother,' replied the pedlar throwing his eyes up towards heaven. 'Is there any decent man amongst ye that will remove this gander from here and bring him to the vet for I'm greatly in dread that 'tis worms he has!'

'You can bet your bloody life that that suit saw a few worms in its day,' said the farmer shifting his cap to the other side of his head. 'I'd swear it came off the back of some poor sailor that was washed in with the tide, may the good Lord have mercy on his soul. Anyone would be afraid to wear what came off the back of a corpse in case he'd be goin' home of a night with a drop in, and the ghost would jump out and tear the suit off him. Take the five pounds and be glad to get it and we'll all say a prayer for the dead man.'

'Well tare-on-acres will ye listen to what that Johnny-the-Eels is sayin',' shouted the pedlar. 'There's no doubt about it but every tinker smells his own fire. The rags you have on you must have come in with a tide, and 'twasn't a spring tide either. If a heavy shower of rain fell on what you're wearin' 'tis how the peelers would arrest you for goin' round naked. The only thing that's good about that piece of a breeches hangin' on you is that it has a long narrow pocket and 'tis hard to get the money out. 'Tis likely your confirmation money is still there and I'd say what coins would leave that pocket in a month wouldn't fill your pipe for you. I'd take a bet that whatever *bothain* you live in the half-door might be there but the big door was lost long ago in a storm. I don't know in heaven's name why a decent man like me is wastin' me time on the likes of you. Here! Give me fifteen pounds and the suit is yours, and I'll throw in a miraculous medal along with it!' At this point a number of onlookers intervened to help make the bargain amid a bedlam of verbal confusion, so I left them to their antics and strolled up the streets of Dingle.

Dingle is a town one cannot help liking. It is a town that has not lost its character. It has had a tremendous resurgence in the past ten years, but it is still Dingle. So many old-world towns have been given a new lease of life over the past ten or fifteen years, but quite a number have lost their individuality. Kinsale is one example, where the blow-ins have taken over and have stamped the town with their own brand of shallow-brained, empty-headed superficiality. This has not happened in Dingle. There have been blow-ins, but they have become Dingle people and have made themselves part and parcel of the town. I rambled into a shop selling books and, without pretending who I was or that I had any interests in those directions, I asked about the sale of Irish paperbacks. They were excellent, I was told. Irish paperbacks outsold British paperbacks by about five to one. A possible explanation given was that the tourist, particularly the British tourist, does not want books that he can get in every huckster shop. He wants to know something about the land he visits, its people, its traditions, its songs. English tourists are particularly interested in books about the fight for freedom, British atrocities in Ireland, and such matters, because there is an almost total censorship on these books in England, and they are curious to know what has been done and is being done in their name. Fiction is not so popular. Modern poetry just does not sell, except to an occasional beardie. John B. Keane is most sought after, and his books outsell those of all other Irish authors. I left the shop, well pleased, and strolled around mingling with the gay cosmopolitan crowd. I rambled along to have a look at the Protestant church which was built on the site of an old Augustinian abbey. When the Augustinians came they were given the pastoral care of the Dingle parish which had long been in the hands of the seculars. Like every new brush the Augustinians swept clean so much so, that the inhabitants went on strike and refused *en masse* to attend to their religious duties. They kicked up such a row that the Pope had to excommunicate the entire town before they finally gave in. In the graveyard nearby is the oldest headstone in Dingle dated 1504. Across the road is Benner's Hotel, which, before it became a hotel in the distant past, was owned by one Simon McKenna, and was the headquarters and principal warehouse of the thriving smuggling business for which Dingle was famous. A well-known Dingle smuggler by the name of Connor was caught red-handed with forty horses, each laden with three bales of smuggled tobacco, by a customs officer named Flood who in his spare time was a bit of an amateur Shakespearean actor, a fowl-stealer, and a playboy. When the case came to court Connor was defended by the great Daniel O'Connell. Flood turned up slightly drunk and O'Connell seizing the opportunity threw several Shakespearean quotations at him to which Flood dramatically responded. When Flood declaimed of 'the fair Imogene' O'Connell asked him how many fair Imogenes he had in Dingle, and how many chickens he stole for his love-parties. This confused Flood and he rushed towards O'Connell exclaiming 'Romeo, Romeo, wherefore art thou Romeo?' and fell in a heap near counsel's table. The case was quickly dismissed and Connor escaped the fourteen years transportation, which he would undoubtedly have got had he been found guilty. Farther up the street, near Chapel Lane, there is a huge flat stone with several depressions or bowls in it, seemingly used at one time as a holy-water font when the crowds attending Mass were very great. I sat on this uncomfortable stone and made a wish for 'tis said that a stranger will have no luck in Dingle if he doesn't do that. I then went along to have a look at the Catholic presbytery which was once reputed to be the highest house in Dingle. It was owned by a Count Rice, an officer in the Irish Brigade, who seemingly had a deep affection for that silly little empty-head, Maria Antoinette. He drew up a plan to rescue her from prison and bring her to live in Dingle in this big house which he had renovated from top to bottom and furnished in the most expensive French style. The plan was fool-proof and would have worked. But no matter how weak a human being may be, there are always moments in life when that weakness is overcome and greatness reached. Maria Antoinette refused to desert France, or abandon the king, and for this she paid with her life.

Dingle in the eighteenth century was a thriving town with its own currency and coinage, and had an extensive export trade in linen, butter and agricultural goods. But exploitation, and brutality, by the occupying English gradually told their tale, and it continued to decline until it reached its lowest ebb after the famine. 'The Almighty,' said John Mitchel, 'sent the potato blight, but the English sent the famine.' The famine, presided over by Queen Victoria, was part of a plan, a final solution, to obliterate the Irish people from the face of the earth. Dingle was one of the worst hit areas. Thousands were evicted from their little homes and died starving on the streets. Here is a quote from a contemporary source: 'The people are in the most part dying of starvation whilst others are carried off with fever and dysentery. Persons are to be seen at all times going about with plates in their hands collecting money to pay for coffins. There is not in this world a more wretched or more destitute locality than this. The starving people go into the tillage fields and re-dig them in the hope of finding an old rotten potato. The people are dying so fast that many have to be buried without coffins. In some cases the graves are only two feet from the surface and many dead bodies lie in the churchyard for four or five days without being interned.' But the famine failed in its purpose. Four million died, but as many more lived on, to never cease fighting until the last of the oppressors were gone three quarters of a century later. On this beautiful summer day, as I strolled around in the radiant sunshine, it was hard to visualise those far-off days and those millions dying.

During the last war the Irish army had an outpost in Dingle and the Sunday before the troops arrived the good canon felt it was his solemn duty to warn, from the pulpit, all the young girls in the town as to what soldiers were really like. As tactfully as he could he explained that when a soldier accosted a young lady, he was not exactly looking for someone to answer the Rosary. He also gave a short discourse on the theology of rape, saying that, in such cases, the innocent party committed no sin. Some short time later a young Dingle girl, who had been seduced against her will three times by soldiers, was heard to remark to her companions: 'Thanks be to God and his Blessed Mother, I had it three times without committing sin, for the priest said 'twas alright so long as I said "no" when I was doing it.'

I rambled out the Tralee road to visit an almost unknown graveyard near the racecourse and on my way I recalled that, in the last century, a post-boy ran bare-footed along this road every day with the post. Half way to Tralee he met the Tralee post-boy. They exchanged bags and ran back to their respective towns. For this they received a wage of seven shillings per week. The graveyard near the racecourse is well worth a visit, not for its beauty, nor indeed for historical reasons, although it is hundreds of years old, but for its sadness. Like all such graveyards it is hidden away from public view, because it is the last resting place of unbaptised children. As you walk around its ancient headstones, many without a cross, you cannot but be appalled at the blasphemous savagery which condemned innocent little children to be buried here, out of reach of their families and loved ones. All this was done in the name of the gentle Christ who said: *Let the little children come to me for theirs is the kingdom of heaven.* As I walked back the road towards Dingle—the words of that most gifted of Irish poets Michael Walsh ran through my head:

> *With trusted heart I offer them to thee*
> *These little travellers putting out to sea.*

Just as I came to the old Railway Station near the entrance to the Skellig Hotel a car stopped rather suddenly and the driver hailed me. It turned out that he was an old schoolmate of mine whom I hadn't met for thirty years. I joined him in the car and we drove into the hotel grounds. There we left Maxie in the back seat and went into the bar. When two old friends meet there are a hundred things to talk about and a thousand memories to recall. Chatting away there in the bar it was as if I were slipping back over the long years and returning to the days of my boyhood. When you are alone and you look back on your life it is like looking at a funeral moving into the graveyard of a thousand hopes, but when you do it with an old friend there is happiness and even laughter. Things that I thought I had long forgotten came up from the cobwebbed corners of my mind. Faces that time had blotted out sprang to life and became real again. I could almost hear the 'laughing voices of old companions' tumbling out of the past. We complimented each other on how young and well-preserved we both looked, each knowing full well that the other was telling lies. I remembered our school days together and the deep, almost fanatical, love we both had for the Irish language. As the years passed I fell by the wayside, like the leaf off a tree before the wintry wind, but he held on. He became a part of every movement that could help Irish and I followed his career through sporadic newspaper accounts of his activities and indeed sometimes, his angry protests. He still spent his holidays every year in some Irish speaking district and for me, he was almost the embodiment of Terence MacSwiney's dictum that 'not all the armies of all the nations of the earth can break the spirit of one true man, and that man will prevail.' In the end after more than an hour's conversation about other things I came around to the question of the language. 'Is it completely finished?' I asked, 'or is there any hope?'

'That's a hard question to answer,' he replied. 'It all depends on an indefinable quality which you might call the Spirit of the People. If sufficient people wanted it strongly enough it could be revived. Also its revival rests in the hands of the politicians, but they will only react if they see enough votes in it for themselves. At the moment there is only a marginal vote in the Irish language so the politicians have only a marginal interest in it. The last Coalition, in what seems to me the most treacherous act in all our chequered history, abolished compulsory Irish in the hope of getting a few extra votes, but they did it under the guise of helping Irish. They said that they were abolishing compulsory Irish so that the people would love the language and speak more of it; which was like abolishing traffic lights so that motorists would love order and then the traffic would flow more freely. But what is even more interesting is that the Fianna Fail party, who routed the Coalition in the elections, have taken no steps whatever to restore compulsory Irish. That is a measure of their interest. We are now the only nation in the world, where a foreign language is compulsory, but our own native language is not, and this I believe is one of the many reasons European nations secretly despise us. The politicians have accurately assessed the mood of the people which is, there are not enough votes in the language to do anything seriously about it. It is only when those interested enough in Irish speak loud enough and strong enough will anything be done.'

'But if that is so,' I asked, 'why is nothing being done? Surely there are thousands of enthusiasts like yourself all over the country to become a formidable pressure group.'

'Did you ever hear of Henry Ford's Ship of Peace during

the First World War?' he asked and without waiting for a reply continued. 'Ford organised hundreds of the most prominent peace-lovers in the USA to cross the Atlantic in a large ocean-going liner on a mission of peace to Europe, all of which he paid for himself. But half-way through, the project had to be abandoned because practically everyone on board began fighting with everyone else. You see, these Peace People did not really want peace if it interfered with themselves. Very often the most vociferous agitators have only a restricted belief in the causes they fight for and it is the same with many Irish language enthusiasts. They are only partially committed, and over the years astute politicians have played on this with consummate skill. I remember when De Valera came into power in 1932 I was sure I could see a golden hue on the horizon the morning he became president. Indeed the whole nation felt, that at long last, after seven hundred years Ireland was to become free and Gaelic-speaking and the ideals of Pearse and the others who died were to become realities. Well, of course, time proved that those hopes were just a lot of rubbish. De Valera had no serious intention of making Ireland Gaelic-speaking or even free. He was concerned with one thing only, power, and everything else was subservient to that aim. Don't misunderstand me, he would like to see Ireland Gaelic-speaking, but he was not going to do anything about it that would alienate a large block of votes. When the Irish enthusiasts became disillusioned with him having waited for so many years, and began to speak out, he started *Comhdhail Naisunta na Gaedhilge* with state aid and grants, and made it both cumbersome and unwieldy. It was the first red-herring in a long series aimed at keeping the Irish enthusiast quiet. When it became clear that this was unworkable voices were raised again and votes were in danger, so the second red-herring was produced, this time in 1958 a commission. Seven years later there came a White Paper out of which came *Comhairle Comhairliteach na Gaedhilge* and this faded out in 1968. Another red-herring was now produced out of the hat called *Comhairle na Gaedhilge* in 1969 and this ceased in 1974. The last red-herring which is still on the frying-pan is *Bord na Gaedhilge* and if that fizzles out another red-herring will be produced. In twenty years we have had five of them. In the next twenty years we shall probably have five more, and each successive one will plunge the knife deeper into the Irish language and this will go on until there is no Irish language left. Hundreds, and indeed thousands of honest and sincere people worked and co-operated in these schemes only to find out that everything was for nothing and that the politicians were only manipulating them. The Irish language is slowly being suffocated by attractive-looking schemes astutely designed to keep protestors mouths' shut, and to keep up the illusion that something is being done for the language in order not to lose a substantial marginal vote.'

'Well,' I said, 'I have been out of touch for a long time but if you are not being too hard on Dev. and the politicians and if what you say is true, it's frightening. But even at this late stage can anything be done?'

'Yes,' he replied, 'all interested in the language could band together into one strong organisation that would refuse any grants or subsidies from the government. Such an organisation would have to take to the streets in demonstrations, marches and pickets, like the Civil Rights Movements in any country. This would have to be done weekly, monthly, without intermission until the politicians sat up and took notice. There are several examples all over the world of the success of such movements, and there is no earthly reason why it could not work here. But,' he added slowly with a sigh, 'I am getting old and the future now depends upon the youth. I have great hope in the youth. They will never be as easily fooled as we were.'

Evening was closing in and the lights were being switched on around the hotel. We had one last drink together, to celebrate the coming revolution, he said with a roguish smile. As he was going to Dunquin, he gave Maxie and myself a lift and dropped us off at the pier. When I shook his hand and bade him good night I found myself saying in all sincerity: 'I suppose I'm too old too, but if you take to the streets, count me in.'

I picked my steps in the twilight between nets and boxes across the large trawler and on to *Dualla*. I went down below and cooked myself a meal. Almost an hour later I came up on deck to finish a drop of wine and take the air before turning in. The skipper of the trawler was sitting on an upturned fish box smoking his pipe. He enquired where I came from and where I was going and, as usual in such situations, we were soon having an easy casual conversation. He was not from Dingle at all, he said, but from further along the coast. I am always intrigued by the closeness of these men of the sea. 'Further along the coast', could mean anywhere in Ireland, and clearly he was not going to elaborate nor tell me where he came from. He had put into Dingle a few days before for minor repairs to his water-pump, and for major repairs to his nets, which had been cut by a Spanish trawler steaming too close to his stern. 'The lousy bastards,' he said. 'They knew bloody well what they were doing. The skipper, a small yellow little cur, with pockmarks on his face like a field of arse holes, only thumbed his nose when I shouted and waved my fists at him. It will cost me a couple of hundred pounds now to repair the nets.' He had little good to say about the Irish Fisheries Department. Spanish and French trawlers were poaching the whole west coast and in a few years no fisherman will be able to earn a living. It was a hard life, out in all kinds of weather and damn little to show for it. Dingle was a crooked town where you were overcharged for everything. All the other towns were just as bad. The price of fish was low, the cost of diesel too high. Indeed everything he could think of was wrong. For nearly half an hour this unfortunate man did nothing but complain, complain, complain. But no human being on this earth is entirely predictable, and even the most miserable of creatures can at times surprise us with a brilliant flash of humour. As I was stepping into the cabin to go to bed I tried to console him a little. 'Cheer up,' I said, 'maybe you'll have better luck for the rest of the year.'

'Not a hope in hell, me dacent man,' he replied. 'Anything contrary that can happen in this world always happens to me. When good luck is goin' the road it passes my door by. 'Tis how I'm the kind of fellow that if Marilyn Monroe had triplets, and I was one of them, I'd surely be the one to get the bottle!'

I was awakened next morning by Maxie playfully rubbing his cold nose against my drowsy face, impatient for me to get up and bring him ashore. We went for a short quick walk in the sparkling morning sunshine. I was glad that the skipper of the trawler was busy on the pier working with his crew repairing the nets, as I had no mind to listen to another string of misfortunes. I sat out in the cockpit with a plate of grilled bacon, tea and toast and enjoyed my breakfast in the tranquil picturesque surroundings. Dingle Harbour was in its most gracious mood today. The morning sun rose in the east and the whole bay seemed to awake, to stretch, to smile like a jaded beauty in her morning bath. The pier was beginning to come alive with fishermen readying their nets and pots, tourists in their light summer clothes wandering carelessly around. There was not even a puff of wind, and the still calm waters were without a ripple. My memory wandered back to the last time I was here when I was taken out in a rowing boat by an old, weather-beaten, sea-farer for a trip around. He pointed out all the notable places of interest and interspersed his travelogue with a fund of anecdotes. Near the south-west corner of the bay he showed me a beautiful mansion nestling in the trees. "'Tis now a convent of nuns,' he said. 'But in the bad old days of the last century 'twas the home of Lord Ventry. They were a poisonous lot then. Many's the poor housemaid had to raise her skirt for the Lord when the feelin' came over him, for if she refused 'tis how she'd lose her job and maybe get her family evicted from whatever little bit of land they had. Isn't it a quare thing now that 'tis prayers are being said in all the rooms where the whoring used to take place. All these gentry was no good. They walked on those under them as if they was dirt and aped up to those above them as if they was God. When the famine queen, Victoria, I think they called her, visited Killarney, all them quality and their ladies was in one hell of a pucker, every one of them doing their level best to sit on the privy after the queen, but Lord Ventry tipped her personal skivy a tenner and got there first, while the seat was still warm. There was a power of money changed hands that time trying to fit them all on the royal privy. For the rest of his life Lord Ventry never stopped boasting that he was the first. As well as that 'tis said King Albert gave him a present of a gold watch on account of he giving him a cure for the itch. He got it from an old cow-doctor in Dunquin who used to cure goats with it. It must have done the job anyway. As well as that 'twas a Killarney carpenter that made the seat of the privy for the queen. She was very fussy, you know, and wanted it made exactly to size, so she sent over a lady-in-waiting who had the same measurements as herself. The Killarney carpenter made a fine job of it for, don't you see, he was able to have fittin's with the lady-in-waitin'. 'Twas a thick seat and the letters VR had to be carved around the sides. I don't know in the hell what them letters means. I suppose it might be "Very Round".'

Many times since I tried to verify his stories without success. In typical Kerry fashion they have neither been denied nor confirmed. I have looked through some of the biographies of Queen Victoria but could find no reference to Prince Albert's itch being cured by a Dunquin cow-doctor's concoction.

Coming up to midday I started the engine, let go the warps and headed *Dualla* out the channel towards the mouth of the harbour. There was no wind and the sky was cloudless. The fresh sheen of morning still glistened on the waveless sea. My next stop would be the White Strand on the Great Blasket Island, only a short distance of twelve miles away, and a little over two hours cruising time. Whenever I sail alone I am usually frightened and nervous at the start of the journey. Even though the weather was perfect and the forecast good, I could not shake off that strange feeling of apprehension which I knew so well. It got momentarily worse when I cleared Reenbeg Point and found myself in the open Atlantic, but this seemed to be the crisis point and as *Dualla* moved steadily along through the calm soothing waters my uneasiness began to vanish and I settled down to enjoy the happiness of the hour. I once asked a wise old seafaring man why these irrational fears preyed on me. I have never forgotten his reply: 'When you sail alone at sea,' he said, 'you always run the risk of meeting God.' Alone one meditates, one thinks, one looks inside oneself and what one finds there can be quite terrifying.

I kept close to the shore with a careful eye for Crow Rock, and a lesser danger, with the intriguing name of Colleen Oge Rock. The sheer majesty of the cliffs along this coast is both breathtaking and terrifying. Their savage grandeur seems to pierce into the very depths of being and stir up the strangest indefinable sensations. I suppose when a man looks into the face of nature in all its splendour and beauty he really looks into the face of Eternity. Joseph Plunkett must have felt that when he wrote:

> *I see His blood upon the rose*
> *And in the stars the glory of His eyes*
> *His body gleams amid eternal snows*
> *His tears fall from the skies*
> *I see His face in every flower*
> *The thunder and the singing of the birds*
> *Are but His voice – and carven by His power*
> *Rocks are His hidden word.*

These wild cliffs range the whole length of the coast from Dingle to Slea Head, parting only at the opening which marks the entrance to Ventry Harbour. Ventry is a pleasant little haven with two safe anchorages, one just off the village and the other near a lonely little pier on the southern shore. One peculiarity about cruising north of Valentia, and visiting unfrequented harbours, is that people are not too conscious of the ways and customs of yachtsmen. Once, many years ago, in Ventry a group of children commandeered my punt, went aboard *Dualla* and helped themselves to minerals and sweet cake. They must have thought it was the most natural thing in the world to do because, when they returned, they sought me out in the village to thank me and compliment me on the nice boat I had. A different peculiarity about sailing this coast is a kind of magnetic disturbance which upsets the compass and sends it awry. There must be some strange minerals hidden away in those mountains that exert a stronger pull on the needle than magnetic north. This was very noticeable during World War II when German planes lost their direction around this area and many of them crashed. One such plane, that came to grief on the slopes of Mount Brandon, had five survivors who were brought to Cork where they remained for a few weeks before they were transferred to the Curragh. Because I spoke some German I had a lot of contact with them during their stay in Collins barracks and I was surprised to find out that these were normal human beings and not the heel-clicking inhuman ogres that the British propaganda machine had led us to believe. They, on their part, were also somewhat amazed at how friendly disposed we Irish were towards them. When the war was over it became fashionable to say, and indeed to write, that while we were neutral, we were in fact neutral on the Allied side. This seems to me to be a pure myth. During those tragic times my job in the army brought me into almost every town and village in Munster and I have no doubt in my mind that the majority of the Irish people were pro-German inclined. This attitude changed somewhat when America came into the war, but I remember one farmer saying to me 'I hope to God these bloody English will be brought to their feet at last.' This was typical of the mind of a people for whom the Black-and-Tans were of very recent memory. In those days we believed that all the political parties were united in their attitude to neutrality and it came as a rather stunning surprise, when, years later General Mulcahy's private papers became available, to learn that he and many leaders of the Fine Gael party were openly pro-British in their sympathies, and indeed went so far as to declare that if we were invaded by England they would not resist. When De Valera made it quite clear that we would resist any invader, English or otherwise, Mulcahy said: '... then this country is being run by a mad dog.' I think, however, that this was a clear case of the leadership of a political party not knowing what the grass roots felt. Thousands of Fine Gael supporters joined the defence forces and would certainly have honoured their oath and resisted invasion no matter from what quarter.

It is interesting now to look back across the years at the private assessment of the war made by the Irish army in casual conversation around the fireside. They saw it as basically a war between Russia and Germany for the domination of Europe—a war which Russia won. Everything else was a side show. The millions of Allied soldiers who gave their lives to free Poland gave them in vain. This, I think, was a fairly shrewd insight as to what it was all about. But these things are now long past and gone and human beings the world over must surely hope that soldiers of the future will not be so gullible.

Time slipped quickly by on this loveliest of summer days. I rounded Slea Head, standing out in all its dazzling beauty, and waved to the many tourists admiring the world-famous view. I carefully negotiated the tricky passage between Stromboli Rock and Garraun Point and dropped anchor in two fathoms of water at the landing place near the White Strand on the Great Blasket Island.

As I was making fast the chain I suddenly recalled that in this very spot a beautiful young girl, Eileen Nicholls, was drowned, as well as the brave islandman who tried to save her. Eileen was deeply in love with, and engaged to, a young poet who was to join her all too soon, at the wrong end of a British firing squad. That young poet's name was Padraig Pearse.

6

The Great Blasket Island is four miles long by about a mile wide, with an elevated ridge running through its centre like a gigantic spinal cord. In the north east corner the little village of scattered houses nestles in the hospitable shade of the surrounding hills, and sheltered from the great south west gales that sweep with almost routine regularity across the island. Not so very long ago between one hundred and one hundred and fifty people lived there, but now it is deserted and abandoned. They were a unique people, a race all on their own, a close, companionable, community who shared each other's work, minded each other's children, helped each other in need, rejoiced at the birth of new life and wept at the death of an old one. They had no shops, no post office, no church, no police, no nurse or doctor, and most of the time no school. When they needed supplies they had to row in their frail craft across the treacherous Blasket Sound, and then walk several miles to Ballyferriter or Dingle. Sometimes when the storms swept down from the north west and raised wild foaming seas, they were isolated for days or even weeks at a time. They grew their own crops, cut their own turf, sheared their own sheep from which they spun their clothes, milked their few cows. Their needs from the outside world were modest; a bit of tobacco, a few sacks of sugar and flour, the odd pair of boots— most of them went barefooted—and a moderate quantity of tea. Indeed tea was a recent discovery. During the First World War they found chests of it washed up from some wreck, and they did not know what it was. For a long time afterwards they mixed it with cold water and used it to dye their clothes. They spoke only Irish for it was but the odd one that could speak any word of English. Their common denominator was poverty, but there was no crime, no suicides nor broken marriages. Yet despite their destitution there is no similar community in any part of the world I know of that has produced such a wealth of great literature.

Tomas O'Crohan learned how to write Irish when he was forty years old, and then wrote his famous book *An tOileanach*. It was translated by Robin Flower into English under the title *The Islandman*, and subsequently translated into several European languages, and became a world best-seller. *Fiche Blian ag Fas* or, in English, *Twenty Years Agrowing* by Maurice O'Sullivan followed shortly on O'Crohan. Then came Peig Sayers *Autobiography* and her *Reflections of an Old Woman*, Sean O Cearnaigh's *An tOilean a Treigeadh* and Eileen O'Sullivan's beautiful little classic *Letters from the Great Blasket*. There were many other books written by outsiders but all were inspired by the ways of the Blasket people. This output must surely be a world-record for such a tiny community. This little island race suffered famines, evictions, rack-rents, proselytising and persecution, at the hands of the English rulers and survived it all. Yet less than thirty years of native government strangled these brave people, and destroyed forever the culture and heritage they so courageously preserved. There is no one left on the island now. They are all gone and the little homes, that they built stone by stone, are in ruins. What will future generations think of us? In a hundred years time will the history books describe us as the barbaric generation that destroyed in a few decades a people, a culture, a heritage that seven hundred years of oppression failed to annihilate. These sad thoughts were in my mind as I rowed ashore to the little landing place that saw generations of great men come and go, live and die, and that finally saw the last boat load of meagre personal belongings leave the Island for ever. I climbed the gnarled stony path to the top of the cliff. When the weather was stormy and the islanders could not cross the Sound to Mass on a Sunday, the parish clerk in Dunquin hoisted a white sheet visible from the island, to announce that Mass had begun in Dunquin church, and on this very cliff where I was standing, the islanders knelt in rain or storm, and joined in the Mass which was being celebrated across the three miles of stormy sea. I walked up to the straggling village now deserted. Most of the houses were in an advanced stage of desolation, partly roofless with the moss creeping steadily over the eves, the windows with gaping holes like eye-sockets in a skull. The law of the jungle reigned everywhere, overgrown nettles and dark leaves choked the untilled gardens. This little corner, unimportant to the world, once resounded with life and laughter, song and dance. Here the poet Dunleavy composed his verse and recited it to a simple but attentive audience; here too, Tomas O'Crohan and Peig Sayers charmed their listeners with folk tales of Irish heroes of long ago. It was all over now and the sound of their voices lay buried forever beneath these silent ruins. I took the rugged path up the mountainside. It twisted and turned, slowly becoming obliterated by the encroaches of nature until it finally petered out to a mere thread of its former self. I walked on and on, until I was almost at the top of the mountain. There I laid down in the heather and rested. I had Maxie on the lead because I was apprehensive lest he might go chasing rabbits and fall headlong over the dangerous cliffs. I stayed there for a long long time with all kinds of disconnected thoughts rambling through the belfry of my mind. I remembered the first time I ever read about the Blaskets. It was something written in 1795 by the historian of Kerry, Smith. 'The inhabitants,' he said, 'are strong lusty and healthy, what is very surprising neither man, woman or child died on it for the space of forty-five years, although several persons, who, during that period came over to the mainland, fell sick and died, out of the Island.' I remembered the story of the Irish poet Pierce Ferriter, who was on the run and hiding in one of the houses in the village, when it was surrounded by the English soldiers who had landed unnoticed. Pierce himself went out to the door, surrendered and invited the soldiers in. Drinks were produced and while the troopers were enjoying themselves the woman of the house secretly poured water into their muskets. When the time came to leave Pierce made a run for it. The soldiers aimed their guns and pulled the triggers but nothing happened and Pierce got away to his hiding place, an almost inaccessible cave in the cliffs. But the soldiers had another day. A few years later they captured this gentle poet and hung him in Killarney. Once before, when he was hiding in that self-same cave, he wrote a little poem calling on God to pity his loneliness, the only sounds he could hear were a monotonous drop of water from the ceiling and the breaking sea beneath him.

> *A dhia, ta thuas nach truagh leat mise mar atáim*
> *I bhriosún uaigneach is nach mór go bfechim an lá*
> *An braon atá thuas in uchtar lice go hárd*
> *Ag tuitim im chluais is fuaim na tuinne le m'sáil.*

I remembered too the great Oxford professor, Robin Flower, who translated *The Islandman* into English and who wrote a scholarly and beautiful book on the Great Blasket called *The Western Island*. Flower spent most of his holidays here, and when he died he left it in his will that he be cremated and his ashes scattered over the heather. So one wet day in 1948 his daughter, Barbara, arrived with the ashes in a copper box. The entire population met her at the landing place and escorted her to the house of Mary Pats Mickey, where the box was put on the dresser and waked with all due respect; snuff, tobacco, drink, a bit of music and a few songs, including one from Barbara herself. It was how Flower would have wanted it. The following morning everyone turned out again, and the funeral procession moved with the copper box to *Claisacha an Duna*, not far from where I was now sitting, and the ashes were scattered with the wind. Barbara then threw the box into the sea, much to the disappointment of one of the island women, who had a clocking hen, and she hoped to get the box so that the hen could hatch out her chickens in it. It was a great waste of a good box, she thought. As I sat there admiring the wonderful view, the island, the rocks, the mainland, the sea, and beneath me *Dualla* like a little speck in the ocean, I began to muse on why the literature of this little community became so successful all over the world. It seems to me that one reason could well be, that the books they wrote reflected the people to themselves, and were not pitched at any foreign audience. A lot of writing in the last century, and the early years of this one, was written to amuse London drawing-rooms by portraying the Irish as a tribe of comic, drunken buffoons, the begorrah, be Jaysus type. This kind of writing one finds in the works of Lever, Lover, Edgeworth, Gerald Griffin and to a different extent Somerville and Ross. These authors started fashions, moulds, and it has taken a long time to shake them off. They influenced many of the present century writers, who changed the theme slightly, by showing us as a sex-starved, priest-ridden society, and were written to please a foreign readership for whom this was but an up-dating of what they had already been used to reading. Yet none of this writing had any great success. It was as if the readers thought it amusing, but sensed in some indefinable way, that it was phoney. The islanders never heard of any of these writers and therefore were in no way tempted to follow the pattern. Gorki was the only writer who influenced O'Crohan. The island writers wrote about themselves, for themselves. They did not try to cover up faults and failings, but they did not produce caricatures either. What they wrote was not only well written but true, and it seems as if the literary world recognised it as such. Today, nearly fifty years after they were published, these island books are as widely read as they ever were, and there is not the slightest indication of a decline in their popularity.

Literature is a strange thing. There are many who can define it for you but few can tell you what it really is. Today, it has become popular to make obscurity an end in itself, to put the onus on the reader to decipher what the author is trying to say. All this really says is that the author is a man of mediocre mind and very limited ability, who is trying to transfer these traits on to the reader. Some time ago I heard a well known modern poet read one of his compositions. I found it utterly meaningless and senseless. When a rather intelligent member of the audience explained that he could not understand a word of it the poet pompously exclaimed 'that is your fault'. I was very tempted to tell him the story of the young student on the continent who was short of ready cash and who entered for a nationwide poetry competition run by a group of these conceited intellectuals. The student won the prize, collected the much needed cash, and was acclaimed by the critics far and wide, as likely to become one of the greatest poets in the country. Some time later the student ran short of cash again, and this time he wrote an article for one of the Sunday newspapers recounting how he composed the poem. He explained that the rules limited him to 150 words so he took a dictionary, and opened it at random 150 times, and wrote down the first word on the left hand corner of the left hand page. This was the poem that won him such widespread literary acclaim. The editors of the newspaper checked his statement thoroughly and found it to be entirely accurate. A little examination will invariably disclose that these excursions into obscurity are extremely shallow, but as Somerset Maughan once said, 'Fools can always be found to discover a hidden sense in them!' Unlike these pompous, asinine idiots, the writings of the islanders have all the marks of greatness in their simplicity, clarity and richness of expression, and they have rightly been acclaimed as first-rate works in the Irish literature of this century. Their spartan lives of poverty and hunger did not deter them. 'Great men,' said Henry Landeau, 'have little beds!'

Tomas O'Crohan and Maurice O'Sullivan I never met, but I knew Peig Sayers quite well. When she crossed to the mainland to live, I used to visit her from time to time whenever I was in the area. To get to the little hut where she lived you had to pick your steps on slippery stones across a stream. She was then old, blind and bedridden. Her couch was placed in a corner near the open turf fire in a tiny kitchen. She was delighted to receive visitors and she would sit up and pour forth a torrent of brilliant conversation, anecdote and story. Her whole being bubbled with life. I usually brought her a naggin of whiskey and her son, Michael the poet, gave her two egg-cups and put water into one and whiskey into the other. She sipped each cup alternately as she talked. One day I called to see her and found her unusually weak. The German writer, George Rosenstock, who was also a medical doctor, was with me. Peig was barely able to drink her whiskey and water and complained of a bad sore throat. George examined her and I knew from the frown on his face that what he saw was not good. She had advanced cancer of the throat and was dying. Later, as we were leaving, she raised her wonderful head and in a weak feeble voice said: *Ta súil agam nuair a casfhaidhmid ar a céile arís go mbeidh sé i bPalás níos rioghdha na an bothain seo'.* 'I hope that when we meet again it will be in a Palace more royal than this miserable hut.'

I did not notice the time passing as I lay there in the heather, until I felt the first cool breeze of evening as the sun sank down behind the island and left me in the shadows. I walked slowly down the path to the landing-place and rowed out to *Dualla*. I went down into the cabin, cooked a meal, and lay on the bunk for a short nap. When I woke twilight was blending into the darkness. I turned on the radio so as not to miss the weather forecast and went out on deck. The arms of night slowly stole around the little harbour. The stars came out one after the other, and a crescent moon poured a soft yellow light which fused and blended into the sea. The silence was unbroken except for the odd splash of a seal near the rocks or the frightened cry of a seabird that had lost its way. The twinkling lights on the mainland and the dark emptiness of the island, brought home to me my isolation. A strange mood of sadness overwhelmed me and this mood was heightened by a concert of Wagner's mournful music coming over the radio. I suppose in a reflective, lonely atmosphere like this, every man's thoughts plunge that little bit deeper, and turn to the tragic sense of life. I began to think about death.

No man really believes in his own death although he knows it is inevitable. It is like as if he were propelled towards a precipice, and covered up his eyes so that he would not see where he was going. It is always somebody else's accident, somebody else who dies, somebody else's funeral, and never our own. But one day death comes and we simply have to face it and face it alone, because nobody wants to share it with us. We do not know what is beyond the grave since no soul has ever come back to tell us, and we can only use our God-given intelligence to speculate. Lazarus and the Widow's Son are the only two recorded cases and they have been peculiarly reticent about their experiences on the other side. When we are gone our friends will be sorry; there will be a funeral which, like all other collective manifestations, such as processions, coronations, inaugurations, is only cheap melodrama. Then as each year passes we will be forgotten bit by bit, until a day comes when nobody will even remember or care. But is this the end of everything? Is this what we yearn for? Is this total annihilation? I doubt it very much. We are prone to seeing ourselves as having a body and soul, but I do not think such is the case. I believe that we are purely a soul which has to operate through a body, with all its limitations, and death is the total destruction of that body only. I suppose you could put it another way and say, that the individual dies but the person lives on. I cannot say that I have been deeply impressed by the arguments of philosophers or theologians on after-life; the best philosophers I ever knew were the country people among whom I grew up. The most convincing case for survival after death was put to me a long time ago by a blacksmith; 'If I am hungry,' he said, 'I know that there is food somewhere to satisfy that hunger. If I am thirsty I know there is water somewhere to satisfy that thirst. There are times in my life when I have a different sort of hunger and thirst, something inside me. I get sad, worried, upset, pained, depressed, and it seems to me that there must be somewhere, where that class of emptiness inside in me is filled up. I know it does not happen on this earth so it must happen somewhere else.' That was a very profound reflection from an unlettered man, who did not know that he was giving expression to one of the most fundamental laws of science *What is possible will always realise itself*. Over the past ten years research was carried out in the USA on hundreds of people who were pronounced medically dead, but who revived after a minute or two. Although these people came from different parts of the country, and from varied walks of life, there were two experiences which they all seemed to have had in common; a tremendous sense of beauty and peace, and a desire never to return to this earth.

When I was a young student I made a collection of how famous people died and particularly what their last words were. Napoleon died mumbling, 'Army... Army... head of the Army.' Daniel O'Connell in his last moments hurled abuse across the floor of the House of Commons at his enemies who were starving Ireland to death. Queen Elizabeth, whose hands were stained with the blood of millions, kept screaming, '... time, more time... Oh God! give me a little more time.' Chopin wondered on his death-bed if they would play Mozart in heaven. Charles II's last words were for his mistress. 'Let not poor Nelly starve,' he pleaded. As Sarsfield watched his blood flow on the battlefield of Linden, he cried, 'Oh that this were for Ireland.' Erskine Childers shook hands with each member of the firing squad who executed him. Henry VIII died roaring from the pains of syphilis, and his bloated body burst open in the coffin. Balzac and Proust, in their last moments, chatted with the characters they had created in their novels. The last words of Hebbel, the German dramatist were: 'The man I am greets mournfully the man I might have been.' But perhaps the best of all was a county man of my own, Cut Quinlan. Cut was the executioner for the Fenians and the Whiteboys, and he is reported to have shot several landlords and their agents during the course of his life. A few times he was put on trial but had to be acquitted for lack of evidence. On his death-bed the priest asked him the customary question: 'Do you forgive all your enemies?' In a feeble voice Cut spoke proudly what were to be his last words. 'I have no enemies, Father, I shot them all.'

The concert of heavy sad Wagnerian music came to an end and appropriately enough a selection of jigs, reels and Irish melodies followed. This changed my mood with some suddenness, and I began to think that if heaven is the fulfilment of every man's dreams and hopes, if he experiences again those moments of happiness he had in this world, then surely in some quiet backwater of paradise there will be a quaint, thatched farmyard pub, with ducks, drakes, hens and chickens around and about the place. In deference to St Peter there will be no cocks—he is a little touchy about cocks crowing. Inside there will be a stone floor, an open turf fire, *sugán* chairs, deal tables, a grandfather clock ticking away, and pictures of the Sacred Heart, Robert Emmet, John F. Kennedy and the Pope hanging on the whitewashed walls. There will be no TV, no piped music or no juke-box. On the dresser there will be a melodian for anyone who has a mind to play, and at the far wall a small short counter. If ever I get there I know I will meet old friends of my cruising days, and their friends too, and indeed many I heard tell of but never met. There will be song and dance and yarn and story. Murphy, the millionaire with the hedge-school education, will be giving advice to all and sundry on how to sell the same load of turnips six times over to the British army, and get paid for it six times too. His most ardent listener will be poor Judas, who always had an interest for turning an honest penny, and who got into heaven because he repented his moment of failure with his life. St Peter nearly didn't let him in, because he mistook him at first for a property developer who lost his way and was travelling in the wrong direction. Connie Coorloon will give us a short recital of his wind-breaking melodies but out of respect for the sacred precincts, he is unlikely to play *Three Blind Mice* and will probably content himself with some devotional hymns like

Onward Christian Soldiers or *Nearer My God to Thee*, although if he took a little too much drink he might forget himself and play *The Wind that Shakes the Barley*. Larry the Liar will be drinking in a corner with Kruger Kavanagh, surrounded by a crowd of open-mouthed angels gazing in wonderment at these two princes of the imagination. Krueger will be telling the story of the conger eel and the goat during the storm at Slea Head, and Larry will recount once more how he came to spend the three months in jail. They will have a friendly competition to see who can tell the tallest story, and although Kruger will have some delightful tales, I'll put my money on Larry. The drunken cattle-drover who sent me to the wrong funeral, causing so much embarrassment to Mr De Valera, will be a new man, because the money that was stolen from him in the eatin' house in Tralee will have been given back a thousand fold. He can now afford the best stallion in all heaven, a magnificent charger that was once one of the four horses of the Apocalypse. He can now spend his days happily servicing all the mares in the Elysian Fields, and he need have no worry he will ever be tempted again to marry. Theophilus, dapper as ever, will be there complete with shaving brush, mug and razor, ready to attend to the urgent demands of any of the old prophets who have a little problem. Already, he will have acquitted himself creditably in his ministrations to the needs of Habakkuk, Elias and even the great Moses himself, who was supposed to have let the Ten Commandments fall on Mount Sinai on account of getting a sudden dart of pain in that quarter. He will have a very special drink with the cow-doctor from Dunquin, who fixed up Prince Albert, and who now proudly wears Lord Ventry's gold watch. Together they will enjoy comparing notes on how best to relieve the aching problem of poor human nature. The fisherman I met in Dingle will have left behind all his misery and depression, and will be drinking, in a romantic snug little corner, with Marilyn Munroe. Everyone will know by the sheepish grin on his face that he's expecting much more than a bottle before the night is out. Sheila, to whom I lost my heart in Valentia, will be radiant in all her beauty, but I am afraid she will have no eyes for me at all. She will be happily reunited with her husband and child. I feel sure St Joseph will drop in for a pint of ale after his day's work, and will sit down alongside the carpenter from Killarney who so expertly constructed that little seat which made Queen Victoria's stay in Kerry so memorable. Poor Joseph will ask the Killarney man for his opinion on a little matter which has been worrying him ever since he left Nazareth. He once made an asses cart for the Sons of Zebedee, and although he measured everything carefully and slowly, twice over, yet when the cart was finished, there were thirteen spokes in one wheel and only twelve in the other. He could never figure out what happened and he corners every carpenter that comes to heaven, but none seem to know what went wrong. St Francis of Assisi will be sure to call, in his ragged, threadbare, brown habit, followed by an army of stray dogs and cats, and Maxie will jump onto his lap and lick his beard, because they have been old friends for a long time. On this earth we are not able to see the saints but dogs and cats are. It will be a gay company, some chatting, some singing, some playing music and there we will spend the evening together, an evening of laughter, contentment and happiness with not a care in the world.

You don't believe a single word of what I have been saying? You don't believe there could be a pub in heaven? That's because you're too used to hearing people praying for the dead; 'Eternal rest grant to them, O Lord. Rest in peace etc.' Now open up your gospels and take a closer look and you will find that Christ never promised eternal *rest*. What he promised was eternal *life*, which is a very different thing. And where would you find life at its best better than in a jovial, well-stocked, well-conducted, pub, amongst the gracious, kind-hearted friends such as you have just met.

The concert of Irish music ended and the weather forecast came through. It gave west to south west force three for Fastnet, which would be a reasonably fair wind although it is usually a little less than that forecast. I will have to leave early in the morning because I am going to try to make Castletownbere before nightfall, and it is a sail of ten hours at least. So I will be up at dawn, when the hills free themselves from the darkness of night, and I will take Maxie ashore for a little run. Then I will stow the punt, set the self-steering, up the largest sails I have, break out the anchor, and get under way. I will cook breakfast while I travel, and enjoy it out on deck as the sun rises in the east and the merry dancing waves from the west break in ringlets of foam against *Dualla's* bow. With a little bit of luck I should reach Castletownbere as planned, and if I do I will stay put for a few days, because there is a good chance that the boys will be able to rejoin me and then we can sail away fine and free back to Cork.

The magic of the Kerry coast I will leave behind, but I will have given to every inlet and harbour a little of my heart.

Well, I hope you were able to stay with me right through the cruise and that you have enjoyed it, and particularly enjoyed the company I introduced to you, for they are the salt of the earth. Who knows, maybe there will be another cruise and another book? Perhaps we'll meet up another day, so until then, goodbye.

MORE MERCIER BESTSELLER

THE WIND THAT ROUND THE FASTNET SWEEPS
John M. Feehan

There are moments in the life of every human being when he becomes haunted with the longing to leave behind the turmoil and tension of daily living, to get away from it all and to escape to a clime where true peace can be found. There are many practical reasons why most of us cannot do this so the next best thing is to read the story of one who tried.

John M. Feehan sailed, all by himself, in a small boat around the coast of West Cork in a search for this Land of the Heart's Desire, this Isle of the Blest.

The result is a book which is not only a penetrating spiritual odyssey, but also a magnificent account of the wild rugged coastline, the peaceful harbours, and the strange unique characters he met in this unspoiled corner of Ireland. He writes with great charm, skill, sympathy and a mischievous roguish humour often at his own expense. His sharp eye misses nothing. He sees the mystery, the beauty and the sense of wonder in ordinary things, and brings each situation to life so that the reader feels almost physically present during every moment of the cruise.

There is something for everyone in this book which is sure to bring joy and happiness to readers of all ages. It is a book that can be read again and again.

'... *brilliant... the Irish Story of San Michele.*' —

John B. Keane

TOMORROW TO BE BRAVE
John M. Feehan

This is the story of a remarkable and wonderful woman who knew she was going to die a lingering and painful death but who faced up to it with unbelievable courage and who turned her last terrible years on this earth into the greatest years of her life—years of kindness, patience, understanding and unselfishness.

The book starts with her death. We share the anguish of her husband, the author John M. Feehan, lonely, bewildered, angrily rebelling agains the unthinkable blow that—like all of us in such situations—he could never believe would really fall. He tells of their early days together; how they weathered the usual joys and sorrows of young married people; how in middle age they began to cast their eyes forward to the time they would enjoy growing old together—and how one day they found out that there was, after all, to be no tomorrow for them. Mary had cancer. She had four years to live. Her husband tells in sober detail of those last four years together when every moment was heightened by the knowledge that their happiness was built of months, then of weeks, and at last only of days and hours. He succeeds in penetrating her inner life, and explains what made her so noble, so cheerful, so selfish—and indeed so happy—while she was knowingly living under the shadow of death.

As he wrote this book, recalling and reliving their years together, John M. Feehan attained the serenity, the mood of acceptance, that Mary knew he would find. At the same time he has achieved a portrait of an extraordinary woman; poignant and truthful, but never sentimental.

IN WEST KERRY
John M. Synge

The most exciting way to learn about West Kerry is to see it through the eyes of one of Ireland's greatest dramatists, J. M. Synge, and to let it weave its magic spell over us. He shows us the splendour of Kerry as we visit Dingle, Smerick Harbour, Sybil Ferriter's Castle, the Great Blasket, Tralee, and we spend some time at the greatest event in Kerry—Puck Fair.

Synge invites us into the huts and cottages of the essentially Irish characters who had a dignity and settled peace that he not only noted but envied. According to Daniel Corkery Synge preferred the happy-go-lucky folks who were not authorities on anything and their rambling stories that had not a word of truth in them to the pronouncements of the wise. Their companionship brings an unwonted delight and we relish the warmth of their hearts, their bright eyes, their reckless and astounding talk as they lead us far away from the stifling streets of the cities and towns. We joyfully go with them over the hillsides, into the mountainy glens and across the bogs.

It is a little star-dust caught, a segment of the rainbow which I have clutched.

LETTERS FROM THE GREAT BLASKET
Eibhlis Ni Shuilleabhain

This selection of *Letters from the Great Blasket*, for the most part written by Eibhlis Ni Shuilleabhain of the island to George Chambers in London, covers a period of over twenty years. Eibhlis married Sean O Criomhthain a son of Tomas O Criomhthain, *An tOileanach (The Islandman)*. On her marriage she lived in the same house as the Islandman and nursed him during the last years of his life which are described in the letters. Incidentally, the collection includes what must be an unique specimen of the Islandman's writing in English in the form of a letter expressing his goodwill towards Chambers.

Beginning in 1931 when the island was still a place where one might marry and raise a family (if only for certain exile in America) the letters end in 1951 with the author herself in exile on the mainland and 'the old folk of the island scattering to their graves.' By the time Eibhlis left the Blasket in July 1942 the island school had already closed and the three remaining pupils 'left to run wild with the rabbits.'

It must be remembered when reading these letters that they were written in a language foreign to Eibhlis whose native language was Irish. Only very minor changes were thought desirable in the letters and these in the interests of intelligibility. Here through the struggling idiom and laboured passages, emerges in fascinating detail a strange and different way of life as seen unconsciously through the eyes of a woman. This is not the island of the summer visitor but one intimately known, loved and feared—and finally abandoned.

THE MAN FROM CAPE CLEAR
Conchúr Ó Siocháin

Conchúr Ó Siocháin lived all his days on Cape Clear, the southern outpost of an old and deep-rooted civilisation. He lived as a farmer and a fisherman and his story vividly portrays life on that island which has Fastnet Rock as its nearest neighbour. He was a gifted storyteller, a craftsman and a discerning folklorist. Here he tells of life on the island drawing on the ancient traditions and the tales handed down from the dim past. There is a sense of humour, precision and a great sense of community on every page.

* * * * *

The Man from Cape Clear is a collection of memories and musings, topography and tales, and contains a fund of seafaring yarns not to be found elsewhere. It discloses aspects of insular life which should delight the inner eye of the world at large and enrich every Irishman's grasp of his heritage.

SEX AND MARRIAGE IN ANCIENT IRELAND
Patrick C. Power

There is a great curiosity today which seeks to see Ireland's past as it really was and here for the first time is a refreshing and stirring book on the sexual mores and laws governing marriage in ancient Ireland.

The Norman king, Henry II, came to Ireland in the twelfth century with the intention of converting the decadent Irish to the 'True Faith'. What type of society had he come to convert? The outside accepted view was that the Irish people were near savages and that their marriage customs caused them to be regarded as incestuous, so that the invasion, in the eyes of the invaders, was in the nature of God's work, to redeem the people from their abominations and iniquities. This book endeavours to throw some light on the attitudes of the native pre-christian and early christian society to sex and marriage. Just how liberal and humane these old laws were, may surprise the reader and it is note-worthy that the christian church failed to have their 'official' laws regarding sex and marriage introduced for centuries.

Dr Power quotes from the Brehon laws and these are a revelation for anyone thinking that our modern Irish attitudes to sexual and marital affairs are somehow those of our ancestors. Nothing could be further from the truth, as most of our attitudes now, and perhaps most of our modes of thought, derive from the invading rather than from the native culture. It seems as if the legislators of Ireland today could learn something from the lenient and benevolent legal system of our pre-Norman ancestors.

www.ingramcontent.com/pod-product-compliance
Lightning Source LLC
Chambersburg PA
CBHW070504100426
42743CB00010B/1751